WHO'S YOUR MUMMY?

ALEXIS DUNSTAN

Who's Your Mummy
Copyright © 2021 Alexis Dunstan
First published in 2021

ISBN
Hardcase – 978-1-922456-51-9
Paperback – 978-1-922456-52-6
Ebook – 978-1-922456-53-3

All rights reserved. No part of this book may be reproduced, stored in a retrieval system, or transmitted by any means (electronic, mechanical, photocopying, recording, or otherwise) without written permission from the author.

Because of the dynamic nature of the Internet, any web addresses or links contained in this book may have changed since publication and may no longer be valid. The information in this book is based on the author's experiences and opinions. The views expressed in this book are solely those of the author and do not necessarily reflect the views of the publisher; the publisher hereby disclaims any responsibility for them.

The author of this book does not dispense any form of medical, legal, financial, or technical advice either directly or indirectly. The intent of the author is solely to provide information of a general nature to help you in your quest for personal development and growth. In the event you use any of the information in this book, the author and the publisher assume no responsibility for your actions. If any form of expert assistance is required, the services of a competent professional should be sought.

Publishing information
Publishing, design, and production facilitated by Passionpreneur Publishing,
A division of Passionpreneur Organization Pty Ltd, ABN: 48640637529

www.PassionpreneurPublishing.com
Melbourne, VIC | Australia

This book is dedicated to my husband, Adrian, and our sons, Zac and Dane.

Contents

Introduction	1
Chapter 1: Fear Less	9
Chapter 2: Mastering Boardrooms and Nursery Rooms	21
Chapter 3: Every Mummy Hurts, *sometimes*	31
Chapter 4: Making Connections	65
Chapter 5: Golden Goals for Golden Girls	81
Chapter 6: Good and Toxic	95
Chapter 7: The Rise of the Guilt-Free Mummy	115
Chapter 8: Cha-Cha Changes	131
Chapter 9: Career Transitions and Life Gems	147
Chapter 10: Boss Mum	161
Chapter 11: Conclusion	173
Acknowledgements	177

Introduction

Even today, in the year 2021, despite all the advancements humanity has made, the ugly fact remains that there is still inequality between men and women in terms of career and family responsibilities.

It is still common for a woman to have to choose between her career and motherhood. Furthermore, it is still believed that women cannot achieve a balanced life taking care of these two responsibilities at the same time, and that in order to live in harmony, one of these has to be prioritised over the other. This may lead to feelings of regret for some women when, later in life, they examine the outcomes of their decisions that led them to choose one of these two.

The idea that these are mutually exclusive and that one must take priority over the other is a misconception. Women can and do live the lives they love without having to choose between motherhood and career.

I can prove to you that a career woman can balance both her career and motherhood at the same time and live a life without having to wonder about "what if" or, worse still, regret the decision she has made. I want to share with you how I and other career mums did this so that you may be inspired to do so too.

There is a plethora of baby books available in the market to prepare mums for the arrival of a baby. However, there are not as many books that prepare mums for the physical, psychological and spiritual journey from career woman to mummy and "career mum". While there are women who transition to career mum without fuss, other women need guidance to navigate the changes required to transition from mum to career mum.

I have coached several career mums in preparation for their return to work. Although it may appear simple, the transition from mum to career mum poses some of the most challenging lessons that a mother will most likely experience in her lifetime.

There are a number of reasons for this, and the three that stand-out above the others are the lack of community awareness regarding the issues faced by return-to-work mothers, the often limited support networks outside of the immediate family that can empower mums to return to work knowing that her baby will be in safe hands, and the affordability and accessibility of childcare. In knowing this, I have devoted my coaching expertise towards coaching career mums. Although we may not yet have all the solutions to these global issues, continuing to increase awareness will contribute towards strengthening these provisions for the future working mother.

As I continue to support return-to-work mothers to successfully integrate back into business, especially after maternity leave, I am conscious of the fact that this is a period in time where return-to-work mothers are typically at their most vulnerable as they experience significant changes to their environment at home and at the workplace.

It is interesting to note, companies invest significant resources towards talent acquisition and the onboarding of new employees. Onboarding programs typically include hours of presentations about the organisation and fancy company-branded materials that are designed to entice feelings of welcome and belonging, with a view that the new employee will remain committed to the company and positively contribute towards its goals.

However, there are currently limited provisions for onboarding, or more appropriately "reboarding", programs for our colleagues who return to work from maternity leave. For some career mums, returning to work from maternity leave is like being a new employee again – one who comes with the added advantage of prior company knowledge and motivation to deliver excellent outcomes. Due to a lack of awareness, some companies inadvertently disengage career mums when they fail to pay attention to the needs of these employees. These needs are not only about reduced working hours or flexibility to work remotely. The most common desires of the career mums that I have coached are to feel welcomed back at work and to feel included – these needs are similar to that of a new starter in the company. If these primary needs are ignored, it is likely to result in lower engagement levels and higher attrition rates for this employee group.

My mother-in-law once told me that being pregnant and giving birth is the easy part. The hard work comes along when the mum has to continue succeeding despite the rapid changes in her world. She now has her beautiful baby that she's responsible for, and at the same time, she also has to take the lead in her own personal transformation.

The changes that take place in a woman's life that allow her to transform from career woman to mum are less understood because it is not often discussed. It is considered personal information that is not for sharing with others. It is therefore not surprising that support networks for career mums tend to be fragmented and many women are left to navigate the changes on their own. The outcome of navigating these changes in isolation is that some mums are left feeling lonely. When they are able to accept and understand that the change is inevitable and many career mums experience the same changes in varying degrees and timeframes, the veil of loneliness may be lifted.

For example, it is common for a new mum to not know what questions to ask and how to approach situations in the way that she did before being a mum. This indecisive manner makes it difficult to focus on their return-to-work plans as overwhelming feelings and emotions may bring out a sense of being out of control. Once they are able to understand their feelings, the ability to focus on planning for the future returns.

When their plans for their future exclude their baby, feelings of guilt for not wanting to be a full-time mum may surface. This guilt can make some mums believe that their goals to return to work make them less maternal and ungrateful for their baby. Suffice to say that not only is it healthy for mums to have their personal goals that do not always include their baby, it is also healthy for their baby to have a mum that is looking after herself in a positive way.

If you experience feelings of guilt, you have the power to release yourself from this guilt-cycle and believe that your aspirations can be exclusive to you. Your thoughts are yours alone and your aspirations make you human. Therefore, some women will enjoy a life of being a full-time mum, while others will prefer to return to work – to each, her own.

Preparation is the key to most success stories. Returning to work after having a baby requires a lot of focus, planning and goal setting.

There are many success stories of return-to-work mums who achieve their career goals and just as many stories of career disappointments. Some of these disappointing outcomes can be attributed to lack of preparation and unrealistic expectations. Therefore, it is important to know that being prepared for the changes that will be experienced in the first few years of the baby's life while managing career goals is critical in safeguarding the happiness and emotional safety of all career mums.

Do you believe that you have all it takes to lead motherhood and your career at the same time? If you answered "yes", then you are one of the few women who would say this, and for that, I celebrate you. If you have doubts about how you would go about this, it's okay, because this is why I'm here for you – to guide you and explore what's in store for you so that you can reap the rewards that you deserve.

This book is a combination of stories from career

mums. What you will read are accounts of what they experienced through their journey. When you have very little time to ponder any future role beyond being a mum, you will understand that the responsibilities are deep, but can result in a beautiful experience if you allow yourself to accept that these challenges will make you a more powerful person, which will benefit not only you but everyone else around you.

As you read along, you will learn how to manage motherhood and your career at the same time, without having to compromise on the quality and satisfaction that you get out of life. The stories of other career mums who have expertly navigated this terrain are your map to success. Through these stories, you will gain the skills to focus your mind, body and soul towards what it is you want and how to bring your vision to life.

The outcome will be living as your best self all the time.

I am a career mum. I am a mother of two boys, a wife, a sister, a friend, and an international Coach and Human Resources Leader. I bring both hands-on and commercial experience to this book.

Before you begin the journey, let me tell you, there will be many changes a career woman will encounter when the baby arrives, and some of these changes could impact you both positively and negatively. The one thing we can all agree on is that there will be some challenges. The longer we ignore the challenges that may surface, the more mothers there will be who fail to live as their best selves. You deserve to be your best self.

This book is not a theoretical study on the postpartum process or feeding routines for your baby. There are already plenty of these books available in the market.

This book is unique. It provides an insight into the juxtaposition of motherhood and career, which is rarely discussed.

So, do you consider yourself a career mum or a soon-to-be career mum? Congratulations. Now, let's get on with the journey!

Chapter 1

Fear Less

Some doors don't open more than once

"After all, it is written in the stars ... that's what John Lennon wrote in his song 'Woman'," she said.

My aunt was a Beatles fan. An independent woman of the '60s, she had all the albums the Beatles had ever released. The only thing she loved more than the Beatles was to travel the world, and at least once a year, she would take her annual leave and go somewhere she had never been before.

She was a former college professor and a published author. To me, she was my mentor and one of the most accomplished women I have ever known. Not someone who surrounded herself with acquaintances, she preferred a quiet life of ritual with those in her very small inner circle of trust. She and I would speak to each other on the phone every day – sometimes both mornings and evenings. On Saturdays, we would meet at the Queen Victoria Building, and spend the morning window-shopping, followed by lunch and a stroll around the city.

One day, I was at my aunt's house, talking to her in the kitchen. It was a Sunday afternoon. I had popped over for a coffee while my husband looked after the kids at home. I was in a dilemma about accepting a promotion I had been offered, and I knew she would be the right person to ask for advice.

"You know that a lot of other people would be grateful for what you have, right?" she said. "Be happy; be thankful. There are people starving out there, and here you are, complaining about your first-world problems."

"I'm not complaining. I just wanted your opinion on whether or not I should accept the promotion," I defended myself.

"For goodness' sakes! Seriously, what do you think?" She paused and asked me, "You know that there was a fifth Beatle?"

"Really? No, I did not know that. I know there was John Lennon, Paul McCartney, George Harrison, and Ringo Starr," I said, trying to appear knowledgeable on the topic she loved the most.

"Well, there was a fifth one … Pete Best … Anyway,

the point is, who knows what would've happened to Pete if he hadn't given up on the opportunity to work hard and be a Beatle."

My aunt is the love of my life, and she knows it because I tell her every day. She tells me that I am just like her, which is why she can't ever get annoyed with me, even when it's warranted. She did not get married and does not have children because, she said, she loves her freedom too much for such responsibilities.

However, she always wanted me to have more than what she had. She wanted me to get married, and have a loving husband and kids. When I asked her why she would want all of these things for me and not for herself, she said, "First, I'm too old. And, second, I made my bed … It was my decision and I do not regret it. For you – I know you. You wouldn't be fulfilled without a family of your own."

"How do you know that?" I asked.

"What kind of a question is that? You have a family now, so does it really matter?" she said.

"But if I take this promotion, I won't get to see my kids as often as I do now, with the increased travel commitments and the larger management responsibilities spread across the region," I said, returning to the original topic of discussion.

"So, don't accept it. See how far that gets you, Pete!" she said.

She was right, as usual. Why was I using my time and energy to talk myself out of a career opportunity?

I started thinking about accepting my promotion and the positive difference it would make for me and my family.

As I write this book, I look back and know that, at times, I was consumed with irrelevant thoughts and thoughts with zero benefit – a vacuum of ideas – but this routine thinking was addictive. In the past, I would catch myself thinking that I shouldn't do something that would have a positive outcome because I was not good enough to do it. I was convinced that I would fail even before I tried to do it. Some call this the "imposter syndrome". Today, I just call it "useless thinking" and realise that I am better served focusing on positive thoughts and continuous improvements.

Thinking negative thoughts attracts more negative thoughts. It is a cycle that can consume your entire being, if you allow it. Once these thoughts stick to your mind, you become your thoughts – a big, black ball of negative energy, unable to open doors to opportunities. Just like a virus is contagious, so are negative thoughts. And others are susceptible to your energy.

I was filled with fear. *Do I deserve to have it all? What if I am not good enough for this promotion and the company just wants to use me until they find someone better to fill the role? Then I will feel disappointed in myself. Then my kids and my husband will have to live with the negative thinking version of me. Then nobody will happy.* It was a downward spiral of thought.

"I don't want to fail and get disappointed," I said, gathering my thoughts.

"Do whatever is in your power to just enjoy the moment. Don't overthink it. Accept the promotion. You have been given a fantastic opportunity. Do not close the door to opportunity – because some doors don't come with door knobs, so you only get one shot at the opening. The world will not stop turning for you, and this opportunity will go to someone else who knows how to walk into open doors, someone more courageous than you. It's your opportunity now, so don't give up on yourself and give in too easily." she said.

*

I took her advice and accepted the promotion.

I enjoyed the job because I gained a significant amount of experience, plus I got to travel around the country and meet some wonderful people along the way. I believe this promotion set the foundation for later promotions and career opportunities in my life.

Can Fear Be a Friend?
A friend once told me that FEAR is an acronym for False Expectations Appearing Real.

Fear is debilitating. It is the rival of opportunity, but it also serves as a defence mechanism and is an important part of our ability to survive. When balanced with logic, fear can create intelligent outcomes.

Fear + Logical Thinking = Intelligent Outcomes

Even though the result of this formula may not always deliver to expectations, it opens doors to opportunities. I use this formula in my life, and it has given me a practical approach to goal setting.

Today, I have experienced being at the top of my career ladder. I have practised risk-taking by balancing fear and logic, which has resulted in me being able to overcome my fear and increase my confidence. The result of this is that, so far, I have enjoyed every challenging second of my career and have earned my place in many boardrooms without compromising on my family responsibilities.

Dealing with the Negatives
Some say that success is a product of hard work and

luck. Therefore, by design, the path towards success is not linear. We all experience degrees of doubts, pessimism, insecurity, guilt and regret. The main differentiator between those who are successful in life and those who are not is the level of resilience they possess. This resilience has the ability to transform negativity into positive action and enables those who possess it to stand up and run when their worlds are dragging them down to the ground. I choose to stand up against the negativities that try to feed on me.

Doubts: I trust my instincts because I listen to my thoughts and focus on how I feel. Whenever I have doubts, I gather as much information as possible about that particular topic and then assess the risk and reward of the desired action. Once I have gathered my information, I make decisions based on logic and emotions.

Pessimism: I never let a "no" stop me from doing something I know I need to do. My purpose and values are clear and I share my values with the people around me. Pessimism, for me, is usually caused by a lack of motivation about a particular topic. I focus on the benefits of the situation, and if the pessimism persists, I pivot towards another topic that gives me a sense of optimism.

Insecurity: Sometimes I feel like I am not good enough. I remind myself that I am the only one in control of these thoughts and emotions. I am the boss of myself and if I don't feel good about me, it's my issue and something I need to overcome on my own. I meditate to get to the root of the insecurity by exposing the reasons why I feel this way. When I know the answer, I address the issue and deal with it. I practise unconditional positive regard. This means that I believe that everything I have done was done because it was the best course of action at the time. Nobody can take away the power of self-regard.

Regret: Regret is a great teacher. It is a learning opportunity that enables me to avoid the same outcome in the future. Regret helps people to evolve into their best selves. I respect regret, but I wouldn't live with it.

I know that there are many more negativities that can plague the mind, but I would prefer not to dwell on the minutiae of these as the focus is on attracting and retaining positive energies – the energies that allow me to be a positive force on others and have a more fulfilling, passionate life that is true to my desires. It can be your focus too. I am inspired by the sentiment in the poem "Invictus", in which William Ernest Henley wrote, "I am the master of my fate: I am the captain of my soul."

The Gift

I have a gift for you.

Imagine, if you will, a round, shiny crystal ball, its thick glass filled with a swirling, white cloud. Your eyes, unblinking, are fixed to its structure. Your thoughts are locked into its powers. It is daring you to find something within the clouds.

You can see your past, present and future in the clouds. Everything seems perfect!

But let me tell you this. It is not perfect at all. Your crystal ball is flawed.

It only presents you with your desires (what could be). It does not give you the power to activate your desires (how it could be). Activating your desires (the how) happens in the present, and these desires are accomplished in the now and the future.

Your crystal ball only contains your past, your values, your beliefs, your biases and your opinions. It contains everything that shapes the person you were yesterday and are today. As for your future – that is entirely up to you.

Now, slowly lift your crystal ball above your head.

You can feel the cold, smooth surface on your fingers and on the palms of your hands.

With all your strength, smash your crystal ball on the

floor. Hear it shatter into thousands of pieces. Watch the white cloud, once trapped inside your crystal ball, surrounding you with a powerful energy, daring you to activate your desires.

I am your white cloud. I will share with you how I manage to have it all and how I open the doors to the right opportunities and shut out the ones that have zero value.

Where's the Map?

> Alice asked the Cheshire Cat, who was sitting in a tree, "What road do I take?"
> The cat asked, "Where do you want to go?"
> "I don't know," Alice answered.
> "Then," said the cat, "it really doesn't matter, does it?"
> —*Alice's Adventures in Wonderland*, Lewis Carroll

Alice had one map, and it was binary. Her questions were: "Do I go here or there?" "Do I take the high road or the low road?" "Is this right or wrong?"

Reality is not always made out of binary thinking and decisions. Let's get you through this maze of thoughts and crystallise your vision to give you the direction that you are looking for.

Everybody should have more than one map for

everything they want to achieve. The people that think they only need one map can be limited in their thinking, unfulfilled, unsatisfied, and disappointed with the unintended consequences of their decisions. The thoughts and considerations that lead to decisions form the map.

One of the secrets to a fulfilling life is to know that the path is fluid; it is not fixed like concrete. The path is long, short, narrow and wide, but at no point is the map paralysed. The map changes. Therefore, you need plenty of maps – as many as you can create – to continue to navigate the continually evolving universe. Your map is alive. It breathes. It moves. It changes. It grows. It shrinks. It disappears and then reappears again.

"You are the map – your thoughts, your desires, your aspirations, your goals, your soul," my aunt would say. It was she who instilled the values in me and shaped my beliefs. Whenever I have important decisions to make, I hear her voice in my mind, and it makes me smile.

Today, I can say with confidence that I live a life of passion by accepting that everything I do is through my own design. I wholeheartedly support all of my decisions. Some of my actions will turn out exactly as I had planned and others will not. I accept that, with all of my good intentions, I will still make mistakes.

I am not afraid of making mistakes because my intentions are pure. Therefore, mistakes serve to make me a better and stronger person. I read a quote that rock-bottom will teach you lessons that mountain tops never will. To me, life is full of lessons and every mistake can be a learning opportunity, if you believe it can be.

To this end, my life's work and passion are guiding people to be their best selves. I do this with the belief that each person is the expert of themselves and, therefore, has the ability to live the life they choose. Ultimately, when you are your best self, you are fearless, and it feels good!

Chapter 2

Mastering Boardrooms and Nursery Rooms

Behind every great man is a great woman and behind every great woman is herself

When a career woman chooses to embark on motherhood, it is a life-changing decision that requires shedding some of the old wants and needs in preparation for a new life full of unknowns. Despite all the hype of how amazing motherhood is (and it is, indeed), being a mum is hard work, and every mum knows that it is not just the physical and mental challenges but also the emotional ones that can take their toll on health and well-being. Left unchecked, being a career mum can be an overwhelming experience, littered with low self-esteem and challenges in navigating the change process. This is intended to expose what can happen when a career woman has a baby and how to deal with the issues with confidence to increase well-being.

"Career Mums are the Best Mums," read a poster, unceremoniously pinned on the staff noticeboard beside the sink in the staff kitchen.

This message was designed by the marketing department as part of a campaign for International Women's Day, 2017.

Although I believed in this sentiment, it made me remember my journey from boardroom to nursery room and back again.

Going from being a career woman to a mum was a challenging transition for me. I experienced feelings of anxiety, low self-esteem and confusion about being a mum once my baby was born.

I will share these experiences because I want you to be prepared for what it can be like to be a career mum and how to overcome the challenges.

When you are a career mum, the world can be a lonely place, especially while your baby is still very young. You might feel isolated as friends and colleagues might not invite you to after-work socials like before you had your baby. On another note, while your partner heads off to work, you secretly despise him for leaving you at home alone with the baby while he continues to have the freedom to go out of the house and work – *how dare he!* Although, for the most part, the social life does return to normal when you are ready for it.

The first thing you might long for while you are alone, caring for your baby at home, is interacting with other adults. If this is something you desperately crave, call on your family and friends, or go outside for some fresh air and perhaps even join a mothers' group.

Mothers'-group gatherings suit some mothers more than others. I know mothers who have enjoyed the community support while others prefer to stay away from them.

I have coached mothers who have shared their disappointing experiences within their mother's groups. The common theme is that they felt overwhelmed by competition between the mothers. However, when we explored the root of their disappointment, it was because they did not have the confidence to be themselves with the other mothers in the group. Furthermore, their feelings of unnecessary competitions and negative judgements were born from their own perceptions and most likely not intended by the other mothers.

One of my friends recently joined a mother's group and she said,

"Career driven and ambitious are not words mothers

use to describe themselves at a mothers'-group gathering. The reason for this is that a mothers'-group gathering is not considered the appropriate forum to discuss the mother's personal ambitions, and there is an unspoken bias that career mums lack the maternal instincts that is required to raise a happy baby. I could feel them judging me and feeling sorry for my baby – *Poor baby, to have such an ambitious mum will be hard on you. That absent mum should be sterilised.* The prevailing wisdom seems to be that career ambitions should be left in the workplace, and it is considered inappropriate when these are discussed at a mothers'-group meeting."

In my experience, finding a mothers' group to join is a relatively easy task. However, to feel a positive connection to this group of initial strangers is a more complicated proposition. It is challenging when a group of strangers try to establish a bond that would otherwise not exist without the babies. Personalities can collide through differences. Biased thinking, misunderstandings and judgement are to be expected. Knowing that what brings mothers together is the shared experience of motherhood creates common ground despite the differences in culture and values.

Therefore, creating an environment of trust, encouraging open discussions that not only include Avent nipple tips but also the mum's well-being and what we can do more of to support each other during this period in time, is an important ingredient in successfully integrated mothers' groups.

Creating space to talk about the mum's well-being brings a diversity to the topics of discussion, which would have otherwise been focused only on the babies. I was fortunate to have a group of women with me to discuss my feelings of vulnerability as a first-time mum and also my personal ambitions. I believe this helped me to build-up my confidence to grow in my role of mum and, ultimately, enjoy every minute of it.

It is time to denounce the silent yet strong impression that the mother's career ambition robs the child of the mother's full love and affection. This judgement is ill-informed and does not provide a positive outcome.

Everyone should know that negative judgements about those "selfish" career women have the power to inflict pain and damage people. Importantly, it ignores the true meaning of motherhood. That is, to care, to love, to respect and to be loved; to be cared for, to be respected for the decisions she makes, while she rarely seeks anything in return. As a result, she is the best mum, and she needs our support to achieve the high expectations that she has established for herself.

I believe that career ambition is not a selfish notion, and that there are women who live a life of satisfaction because they enjoy balancing motherhood with their career. So, if this makes them feel good, who are we to judge, when we should instead try to understand and support?

I was a member of a number of different mothers' groups. During one of my mothers'-group gatherings, eight weeks post-partum, ready for adult interaction and excited to meet new friends, I arrived at the park early and set up my picnic blanket, with my son by my side.

The gathering started with a round-carpet, meet-and-greet. When it was my turn to introduce myself, I excitedly shared that I had an amazing birth experience and couldn't wait to get back to work once childcare facilities were confirmed. The initial smiles on some the other mothers' faces were replaced with confused looks as to why on earth I would ever want to return to work.

Perhaps I should have been more attentive to my audience before sharing my truth and given them what (*I perceived*) would have made more sense to them; I should have said that that being a stay-at-home mum was the best thing to ever happen to me and my family and that I loved every minute of it. This, however, would not have been true for me.

There were a number of other career mums in my mothers' groups, and the reality is that initially, they did not feel comfortable sharing their career stories during our mothers'-group sessions, despite their career being a significant part of their lives.

I am one of the women who openly shared that I looked forward to continuing my career while I lovingly nursed my newborn baby as we sat on the picnic blanket. I felt the awkward stares to begin with, but as time passed by and we all got to know each other better, our network strengthened, and years down the track, we continue to keep in touch with one another, and are proud of our achievements.

It is considered strength of character for a woman in business to demonstrate ambition and to have the courage to not let anyone or anything get in the way of her career future. Usually, this drive does not come without challenges, but if she passes the tests by demonstrating the required behaviours and deliverables, she will most likely achieve her career goals.

This commitment to achieving your career ambition, when combined with caring for your children, can result in a powerful future. The path has been set by our elders for us to accept that career ambition and motherhood are not mutually exclusive.

You can apply this proposition by acknowledging that you are the sole owner of your thoughts and feelings, so are others of theirs. Therefore, continue to have the confidence to withstand the opinions and judgements that others may have of you because you are the one, true authority of your life.

I believe that all mums are the best mums, and here are a few reminders for all of us:

1. **Fear Less**
   Overcoming fear is necessary in order to live the life that you want. This means that whatever barrier is placed in front of you, fear must be overpowered in order to achieve what is desired.

2. **Mastering Boardrooms and Nursery Rooms**
   Some mothers enjoy balancing motherhood and their career at the same time while other mothers prefer not to focus on their careers while their babies are still very young, or at all. The goal is to respect each other's lifestyle choices and focus on your own satisfaction.

3. **Every Mummy Hurts, *Sometimes***
   Being a mum, it can be easy to forget that love begins with the person staring back at you in the mirror. Self-love is a pure love and a basic need for living a life of satisfaction.

4. **Making Connections**
   Connections are key to your return-to-work success. The support you receive through your

connections will either make or break your return-to-work plans.

5. **Golden Goals for Golden Girls**
Most of us will agree that setting meaningful goals can lead to successful outcomes. I will share some straight-forward tools to empower to bring your goals to life.

6. **Good and Toxic**
Identify and differentiate between the good and the toxic people in life and learn how to be good and avoid being toxic for others.

7. **Rise of the Guilt-free Mummy**
Feeling guilty and unsure about almost everything is common for a lot of new mums. I can tell you that practising self-appreciation will boost your self-esteem.

8. **Cha-cha Changes**
It is often said that change is constant and the speed of change for new mums is on overdrive because not only are mums expected to look after themselves during this process, they also have the added responsibility of looking after their babies. Understanding change and learning to deal with it in a manner that preserves your happiness is important during this period.

9. **Career Transitions and Life Gems**

   You cannot manage what you cannot measure. Your map will determine your decisions and the outcome of your future. Career transitions can happen at any point in time, to anyone. Being prepared for career transitions can cushion the unsettling unknowns by aligning your plans for the future.

10. **Boss Mum**

    How does she manage being a career mum and lead the changes to create successful outcomes?

I will be examining each of these points in detail in further chapters to empower you with the knowledge that you need to support your return-to-work plans.

Before we move on, I'd like to emphasise that career mums are on the rise. We want to remove the negative stigma attached to career mums because we believe that success is for everyone who wants it. And mums are no exception.

Let me guide you on this journey as I share some inspiring stories of love, courage and determination that will prove to you that you can overcome any challenges that life throws at you, especially if you are about to welcome your new baby or care for your children while working hard on your career.

Chapter 3

Every Mummy Hurts, *sometimes*

It's 3 AM

It is rare for a new mother to admit this, yet it is commonly known that one of the first values that a new mum sheds when her baby is born is self-love. The reason for this is that once her baby is born, the expectation she imposes on herself is that everything revolves around the baby. The mum has to take the leading role of primary carer and feeder; she is responsible for the baby's health and well-being.

Through this process of keeping the baby alive, mums lose focus on themselves and transfer everything they have to the baby.

This is why it's safe to say that there's a reason why some mums suffer in silence with post-partum depression, anxiety, loneliness and isolation. However, by lighting a torch on these issues, we are able to support and coach mums in need – to explore deep emotions so that they can bring these feelings out in the open, comfortably discuss them and be empowered to seek clarity for themselves during this confusing period of time.

It's more convenient for others to hear about the joys of motherhood than to listen to a mum sharing her vulnerabilities and about not being able to breathe at 3 AM because of the fear and anxiety that has consumed her life for reasons unknown to her.

If you can expect these issues beforehand, you might be able to prepare yourself in order to lessen or avoid these feelings altogether.

The key is self-love.

Self-love is regard for one's own happiness or advantage and it is as important to the new mum as water is to life.

This is something every mum needs to remember. Of course, it is easier said than done. Some mothers I have coached have realised that their benchmark for happiness was measured by comparing their circumstances to others'. For example, when they see what others have compared to what they have, it can sometimes result in either being grateful for their position in life or dissatisfied with who they are and what they have.

The question remains the same for all. How do you genuinely love yourself when you are not satisfied with who you are?

It is a mirror effect, which is activated when the mum you see in the mirror differs from the type of mum you believe you should be. For example, when you try to fit into who you think you should be, rather than love who you are, you are not living an authentic version of yourself. So how do you love someone you are not? The answer is: you can't.

When you love somebody more than you love yourself, you are not giving that person the love that they deserve and you are not giving yourself the love that you deserve either. So, there is no love there for anybody.

When a woman finds out that she is about to have a baby, she may adopt changes to her lifestyle to create one with a healthier focus. She may abstain from drinking alcohol or she may be more selective about the type of food that she eats. She may exercise more or perhaps less. Ultimately, by looking after the health of her baby, she takes care of herself. However, once the baby is born, all that self-love is transferred to the baby. The mum may ignore her needs, and when this happens for a prolonged period of time, she may suffer in silence because she may not have the required levels of self-awareness to articulate and understand that this is happening to her – confusing, right?

Love yourself, and then you can give love to your baby.

Let me tell you a story. My husband and I had been married for three years before we decided to start our family. We had worked hard to reach satisfactory levels of responsibility within our companies, and, as a result, we achieved a comfortable financial position to start our family. I take comfort in planning my life's activities, and because of this, most things appear to come easily to me; therefore, I didn't expect pregnancy to be any different.

We underestimated the difficulty of getting pregnant. Medically, there was nothing preventing us from conceiving naturally. However, it eluded us for a long time. The longer the process, the more anxious I became and the more I wanted to have my baby.

I signed up for discussion boards with women who, like me, were having difficulty in getting pregnant. Through the online communities, I learned about the depths of desperation that some women go through to have a baby. Although, for the most part, I preferred reading the pregnancy success stories. Each time my periods were late, I would excitedly do the at-home pregnancy test and, even with a negative result, would consult my online friends for affirmation; perhaps they could see a faint positive line that my eyes had missed. Suffice to say, I was obsessed with getting pregnant.

One day, I was in a meeting, and after a sip of coffee, a tidal wave of nausea hit me. I could not tolerate the smell and the taste of this cup of coffee. This was the same instant coffee that I drank every day. Initially, I thought that perhaps the coffee blend had changed, although my unsophisticated palate would not usually be able to discern different types of coffee blends. Instinctively, I knew that I was pregnant.

As soon as I could, I went home and consulted my trusted home-pregnancy tester. Three minutes later, I finally had the two lines that I had been waiting to see for so long. I did not even need to consult my forum friends about the lines, as I could see them clearly. I was pregnant!

I loved myself again. It was a fantastic pregnancy. My skin glowed. My hair shone. Although I couldn't tolerate the smell of lavender, I was ecstatic – I was about to become a mum!

And then, on February 28, my perfect baby was born. As I held him in my arms, I whispered in his ear, "I love you so much. Thank you for choosing me to be your mum. I will always love you."

The day after giving birth, as I lay in my hospital bed, with my baby sleeping peacefully in his cot beside me, my world turned upside down. The realisation that I was alone with my baby and I did not know what to do made me cry.

Why does this happen?

When in a safe and comfortable space of trust, all mums will tell you that babies are demanding and loving themselves post-birth is hard. Most mums can't explain the reasons why it is difficult to focus on loving themselves soon after birth. Are we supposed to continue to believe that self-love should be paused to focus only on the baby? To think otherwise must be wrong. Well, let's destroy this judgement once and for all.

As a baby is born completely helpless and requires the parent to anticipate its every need in order to survive, being a parent is the most important responsibility bestowed upon humans. It is an exhausting experience that tests patience and resilience.

The reason why mums find it difficult to practise self-love post-birth is because of the unexpected lifestyle changes. Once you are aware of these, you will be better equipped to master all the events ahead and to overcome the unexpected.

Let's look into the top lifestyle changes that women

will experience after giving birth and what you can do to address these situations.

1. **Me Time**

    During the first few months after giving birth, you cannot be physically apart from your baby for more than a few minutes (or maybe a couple of hours, if you have someone else babysitting). Your mind will always be on your baby. Is he breathing? Is she too hot? Is he too cold? Has he had enough to eat? Am I doing the right thing? Questions like these will consume your mind and leave little room for any other thoughts to be considered and acted upon.

    I met a new mum the other day; she'd had her first child a few months earlier. She and her husband had been married for four years before the birth of their son. Needless to say, their baby's arrival was a long-awaited dream come true for both of them.

    She told me that before having their baby, she and her husband had agreed that once the baby was born, they would share the responsibilities of childcare equally, meaning she would still be able to go out with her friends and enjoy the Dubai nightlife whenever she pleased.

    However, her plans to continue the lifestyle she

had before having her baby were proving to be unrealistic. Firstly, she was breastfeeding. Therefore, she could not be away from her baby for more than an hour at a time. Secondly, she felt isolated from her group of friends as she was the only one with a baby. Finally, she mourned for the life she once had and missed her freedom the most.

As she sat across the table from me, her baby asleep in his pram, she leaned over and whispered that she was very upset at her husband because his life had not changed at all. He was still going out with his friends, going to the gym whenever he felt like it and didn't seem to care that he was failing at doing an equal share of childcare. Basically, she felt that he was leaving her to do everything for their baby.

She said she had shared her feelings with him and he dismissed her feelings by saying he would do all the things she has to do for their baby **if he could** but he can't.

She told me the only thing she needed was to hear from someone else that she was not insane for thinking that way and that this stage would pass. I told her, in my experience, it's not wrong to reflect on life before being a mum and that she would one day have her "freedom" again. I shared with her a saying that my mother-in-law once told me many years ago: "In motherhood, the days are long but the years go by very quickly. So, enjoy it."

2. Baby Love

Some people may choose not to demonstrate as much interest in your baby as you would expect them to do. This is not a reflection of how they feel about you or your baby; rather, it is a personal choice that they have made during that particular interaction.

Some people believe that children have the ability to bring family and friends together. You may choose to spend more time with acquaintances who have kids and strengthen these relationships as the shared experience of parenthood brings you closer together.

A few years ago, my son attended one of his classmate's fourth birthday party. It was a party where the parents were also invited to enable the parents to socialise and keep an eye on their children.

I knew most of the mothers there as we lived in a small community. However, there was a new family who had recently joined the class and was now at this party.

As I was chatting with my group of parents, the new parents joined in and introduced themselves.

WHO'S YOUR MUMMY?

They were new residents of Dubai and were originally from Toronto, Canada. They had two children. One was four years old – he was playing with my son in the inflatable jumping castle – and the other one was eight months old. She was bobbing her head against her mum's chest, comfortably nestled within her Baby Bjorn sling.

While our group were chatting idly about life in Dubai, our kids and their school, the mum randomly asked me if I would like to carry her baby. I was surprised as to why she would ask me to carry her baby as she had her husband standing beside her. I would've expected him to be a better option than me, a stranger, to hold her baby. Nevertheless, I agreed to nurse her cute little baby and I enjoyed holding her. There's something about the smell of a baby, and I can't resist holding them, given the opportunity.

When her baby started to fidget in my arms, I eagerly handed her back to her mum. At this point, the mum asked another mum in our group if she would like to nurse her baby. The other mum said no so fast that our group laughed.

As the party was coming to an end, the mum with the baby came up to me and asked if we could meet again as she felt a connection with me and wanted friends in her new city.

I told her I would be happy to meet and that our group of mothers met once a week at the community club and she was welcome to join us. She said she would prefer to meet with me only as she didn't feel comfortable with the others in the group, especially since they had laughed at her earlier in the day.

I met up with her on my own, and, eventually, she did feel comfortable spending time with the rest of the group.

The moral of the story is: do not take offence when others do not want to nurse your baby. Your baby doesn't mind if others don't want to nurse them, so neither should you.

3. **Career Ladder**

    Your job might not change, but you will. For the first few weeks, you will survive on very little sleep, which can cause confusion and lack of focus.

    It is important to trust someone else to look after your baby so that you have time to rest and recharge your batteries in order to focus and have a clear mind.

    It is only with clarity of mind that you can plan your return-to-work activities. Once you have developed your return-to-work plan, you will return to work exuding ability and confidence.

In my experience, great places to work actively support return-to-work mums because they know the important contribution that women make in the workplace. Therefore, they tend to invest in employee-centric programs to engage and retain their employees.

Let me tell you a story:

I am an early riser and have always practised a work routine that includes getting to work before my colleagues. This means the car park is usually empty when I arrive to work. One day, as I was preparing to park my car in my usual spot, I noticed that there was a car already parked there. Although I did not have a designated parking spot to my position, I did find it rather surprising that someone else would park in one of the most inconvenient parking spots, considering the office entrance and exits were furthest from this spot. Personally, I parked there in order to avoid damage to my car as my husband has encouraged me to adopt his theory that the more inconvenient the car spot the better because there's less traffic, and less traffic decreases the risk of accidental damage.

When I arrived at my office, I received an email reminder that one of my colleagues was returning to work today after twelve months off on maternity leave. I had a meeting scheduled with her at 10 AM.

I had been with the company for less than twelve months, so I did not know her before she went on maternity leave but I was familiar with her employee file. She had been working in the company for five years. She started off as a Junior Administrator and due to her strong work ethic and performance, she had been promoted twice and was now a Sales Team Leader.

We had a very candid meeting. She talked and I listened. She said that she had considered not returning to work because she felt undervalued even before she went away on maternity leave.

She said that her experience with the company was that people have jobs and not careers. She said the difference is that a job is something that you do to make ends meet and a career is something that you do to the end because you are passionate about what you are doing and it is aligned to your purpose.

As our meeting was approaching the end, she said that she felt relieved that she was able to be vulnerable with me. Her experience during maternity leave had left her feeling confused and very tired. Our meeting made her feel supported and she took comfort in not feeling like she was negatively judged.

Armed with this information, I met with my boss to get approval to incorporate an additional stream into our employee experience strategy: to develop a reboarding program for return-to-work parents (both mothers and fathers). I argued that we needed to design this program because our employees are the most important contributors to the success of the organisation. My boss agreed.

The next morning, I arrived at work to find my usual car spot was vacant. I reversed into my car spot as another car was waiting behind me. I parked my car and was walking to the elevators when a voice called out from behind me asking me to wait. It was the same colleague I had met with the previous morning.

She thanked me again for the meeting and for the prompt action to her feedback. She said that as a new mum, she was nervous about not being heard and wasting her skills with the wrong company. Now she felt that a more promising future with the company was possible because of the attention she had been given as a return-to-work mum. Finally, she said that for the last five years, she was the only "nut" who would park so far away, and that she was happy that there was now another one just like her.

4. **Social Life**
   There will be a decrease in your out-of-home social activities during the first few months (*at least*) of having a baby. Believe it or not, you might not even want to leave your house at all.

   Then, one day, you will courageously get your pram ready and walk out of the door with your baby. This first walk is a massive achievement and heralds more outdoor activities to enjoy.

   Recently, I was invited to participate in a mothers'-group session for new mums. Being a mum of two, they considered me a worthy guest to their group of first-time mums. The topic of the day was socialisation post-partum. We discussed what this means and how important it is to the well-being of the new mums. The general consensus from the group was that immediately after giving birth, it was difficult to be motivated about socialising with others (*close family excluded*) and it felt awkward to socialise with people who were not parents themselves because the topic of conversation was not going to align with the differences in lifestyle between having a baby and not having a baby.

   The points that the group agreed on were that, as new mums, during the first months, they felt a need to isolate themselves with their babies and only spend time with their inner circles. There is no specific reason as to why this was the case but it is not about outlining a definitive point in time when mums "should" socialise. Neither is it about comparing the life experience of motherhood to that of people without children, as previously discussed.

The mums felt that they reached a point in their transformation where they were out of isolation-mode and seeking connections outside of their inner circle. They agreed that this step was an important part of their transformation to empower them to continue to socialise as independent adults.

The outcome of the mothers'-group session was accepting that it is important to socialise with other people as soon as you are comfortable to venture out into the world again. While it may be tempting for some mums to stay within the safety of their own home, away from others, prolonged periods of isolation can lead to loneliness.

5. **Affection & Intimacy**

Whether or not you are recovering from a major C-section or other birthing achievements, you may not feel like being either affectionate or intimate with your significant other (SO). This lack of desire for affection and intimacy soon after birth is not necessarily abnormal. I know some mums who have been overthinking this topic to the detriment of their own well-being. Ultimately, it is okay for a new mum to take her time to feel comfortable in her own skin again.

I speak from experience when I say that pregnancy and giving birth does change most women's bodies in some way. Some of the changes are temporary while others may be more permanent in nature. For example, some women may notice that once their baby is off the breast, their breasts will align closer to their belly-button than their chest. Some women may also notice additional wrinkles on their bodies where they never would've expected wrinkles to appear before having a baby. Some women embrace these changes while others will not.

I often get asked by new mums if their body will go back to how it was before they got pregnant and gave birth and my answer is always the same – "it's up to you and your body".

A friend of mine is one of the bubbliest people in the world; that's why we call her "Champagne" (*not her real name, of course*). When Champagne got pregnant with her third child, an unexpected gift from the heavens, she was so relaxed that she relinquished control to all of her food cravings. Unfortunately for Champagne, her cravings were for high-calorie, sugary sweets. She devoured entire boxes of chocolates at a time, drank litres of chocolate milkshakes and often sent her husband off to the shops, at odd hours, when they ran out of supplies for her insatiable appetite.

In the twelfth week of her pregnancy, her obstetrician informed her that she was at risk of pre-eclampsia and type 2 diabetes due to her significant weight gain. But even this warning was no match for her calorific desires.

At her twentieth-week scan, her obstetrician told her that she "may develop" placenta previa. It is a condition where the baby's placenta covers the cervix. This meant that she was at risk of bleeding, and considering her older age of forty-one, she couldn't afford any bleeding this early into her pregnancy. Therefore, the doctor ordered her to limit her physical activities and rest for most of the day.

Eventually, Champagne delivered a healthy baby girl at thirty-six weeks, via C-section. Along with her new baby, she had also gained an additional 25 kg of weight. Standing at only 160 cm and weighing 85 kg, she was considered overweight.

She said that as soon as she healed from her C-section, she committed to getting back into shape and engaged a personal trainer for three sessions per week. She limited her calorie intake by cutting back on carbohydrates and maintained a healthy balanced diet to ensure she had enough calories and could feed her baby. This was the motivation that she needed to reform her lifestyle and self-esteem.

It took Champagne almost two years after having her baby to get back to her desired body shape and fitness levels.

She told me, "Your body will respond to the attention that you give it." This means that with motivation and perseverance, you have the power to reshape your body and lifestyle. There are many modes of physical transformation platforms that are readily available in the market that promise to deliver amazing results. The rest is up to you, as you need to find the time and energy to focus on your desired outcomes.

6. **Your Significant Other (SO)**
It may be surprising for some, but your SO might not have the same approach in taking care of your baby as you do. He might not know how to soothe your crying baby in less than thirty seconds like you can. He might put the nappy on backwards, and he might not know the ratio of powdered formula to water (even though you've showed him how to do it and the instructions are on the tin).

This disparity in skills is rarely because your SO wants to do less caring for your baby than you do. It is more often because you have a different style of looking after your baby. However, he can be the expert too! If he is unsure, show him how to do baby care. Try not to lose your patience when demonstrating how you want things to be done for your baby and explain why it is important to you. You might also learn that doing things his way is a better option? Importantly, both you and your SO must agree on the level of responsibilities shared between the two of you for taking care of your baby.

Perhaps you could both acknowledge the good things that you are doing for your baby.

When your baby wakes up crying at 3 AM, perhaps you and your SO could agree to take turns getting out of bed to soothe your baby back to a peaceful slumber.

However, when you give your SO the responsibility of looking after your baby on his own, trust him to do it his own way. Do not be tempted to over-prescribe how he should do it, as he may have his own natural style that works better for him and your baby.

I never expected that the initial months of being a new mum would be such a challenging experience for me. I thought that I would be confident and knowledgeable in everything about my baby. The reality is that, back then, I was not. There was a point in time when I felt like I had failed because I didn't end up being the expert mum that I imagined I would be. Now, I know that I overcame these challenges by accepting my truth – that looking after my newborn baby was difficult but the challenges wouldn't last long and the rewards were amazing.

Two Sides of the Coin

One of the most personal questions you could ask a mum is why they wanted to be one.

Usually, the responses are: "I didn't plan to be," or, "I wanted to start a family because I couldn't imagine my life being complete without having children of my own," or to the extreme, "Because my husband/SO would have left me if we didn't have children."

The other side of the coin is, "Why didn't you want to become a mum?"

Usually, the responses are: "I love my freedom too much," or, "There are enough people in the world," or, "Kids are hard work. Not my cup of tea, thank you very much."

These two questions, with different responses, provide an insight into self-love and what happens subconsciously to mums.

The experience of pregnancy and giving birth is mostly different for everyone. However, as soon as the mum holds her newborn baby for the first time, the feelings of love for her new baby now cradled in her arms is a beautiful experience for all mums.

You might whisper into baby's ear, "I love you. I will always love you. Thank you for being here."

You might experience tears of joy brought on by the chemicals in your brain going into overdrive. You might laugh and cry at the same time as you wrestle with your emotions, realising the enormity of your achievement – giving birth to a human being. Your SO might be holding the camera to capture these precious moments. Right here, at this point, your self-love must continue and be shared with your baby – do not be tempted to forget this.

My Experience with Post-Partum Anxiety
In preparation for having my baby, I read all the baby books I could find to increase my knowledge about motherhood. I was motivated to become the expert mum for my baby.

From what happens to your body during pregnancy, to how to furnish your home for baby, baby sleep and feed schedules to baby personality and well-being, I thought I had all the information I needed and therefore was ready for my baby.

Every Mummy Hurts, sometimes

My firstborn was the perfect baby. He fed like a champion, responded to routine, and, above all, he was healthy. To the outside world looking in, I had everything under control. A perfect little family with the perfect little baby must equal a confident mum.

Even though I may have appeared confident, I realise now that my self-esteem was very low. Despite this, every morning, I got ready for the day in the same manner I did before having a baby. Needless to say, my outward appearances did not match my internal struggles. As for my baby, I dressed him in his cute baby outfits and prepared our supplies for our daily outings. I did all the things that I read about in my baby books; everything that a perfect mum would do.

As I joined the other mothers in my mothers' group, smiling and sipping café lattes at the park, inside, I was hiding a secret. In reality, I was a crumbling mess. Riddled with anxiety, afraid to go out, afraid of the dark, at times unable to breathe and afraid to be alone with my son because I didn't know how to look after him on my own.

I still remember one day, at 6:45 AM, my husband was ready to leave for work. Our son was asleep in his cot beside our bed. My husband leaned over to kiss me goodbye.

I remember feeling a bolt of sharp pain in my chest. I could not breathe. I sat up and placed both my hands over my chest, frantically gasping for air. My husband was stunned. We both knew something was wrong, and it wasn't my breathing.

A few days after this incident, I was diagnosed with post-partum anxiety.

I had placed a lot of expectations on myself about the type of mum I had to be, and when I couldn't meet my own expectations, my anxiety levels peaked.

Here are some thoughts that went through my mind as I battled with post-partum anxiety:

1. **I'm a bad mum.**
   It is said that human milk is the best for human babies and any other alternative is profoundly inferior. I believed it too, but when I got mastitis, the physical pain was intolerable. However, the disappointment of not being able to give the best to my baby was worse.

   I persevered through the pain, until my breasts became so engorged that I had to pay a visit to my doctor and was prescribed antibiotics. During this time, most nights, I cried myself to sleep and hated myself for having to feed my son baby formula.

   Eventually, my mastitis cleared and my son didn't mind his formula. However, the feelings of failure took longer for me to absorb because I forced myself to believe that I had failed this basic responsibility of feeding my son.

I was envious of the other mums who were breastfeeding while I had my formula bottles.

Eventually, I allowed myself to accept that there are things outside of my control that do not have the power to supersede my achievements as a mum.

I believe that all mums have the best intentions for their babies and those who do not have other issues and may need medical professionals to assist or intervene.

In my wisdom, I know that every mum is different. The differences in culture, values, approach, lifestyle, desires and expectations make it unnecessary for anyone to produce a one-size-fits-all guide for motherhood. So, motherhood is not about implementing a benchmark for success and rating systems that measure good mum versus bad mum; rather, it is about empowering all mums to be the best mum she knows how to be. We can start by reminding every mum that her authentic self is the best self and the only self she needs to be. It is through living with authenticity that true love is shared. Regardless of who you are and what you do.

2. **I will hurt my son.**
   I remember during the first few weeks of being with my newborn son, I was paralysed by fear and uncertainty. These feelings caused irrational thoughts to plague my mind. I feared that I would do something wrong and end up harming my son. This fear led me to be overly cautious and unsure about everything I did. It destroyed my confidence to the point where I was unable to walk more than two steps without checking to make sure that my son was still breathing.

   I was nervous to transition him from a liquid diet to solid food for fear that he would choke on anything firmer than mush. Under our paediatrician's supervision, I eventually gained the confidence to introduce solid food, but even with this intervention, it was a frightening experience at first.

   It was difficult to be incredibly insecure and, at the same time, try to act with confidence in front of others. On the one hand, I was afraid to be alone with my son because I did not have the confidence in myself to look after him alone, and on the other hand, I had to pretend to have everything under control. For example, because of my irrational fears about my son's health and safety, I had installed baby monitors in all rooms of our house (except for the bathrooms) so I could monitor his every breath and watch his every move, at all times.

During this time, my husband did not judge me for my irrational behaviours. He held my hands when I wanted him close and also gave me space whenever I needed it. He knew that this period was part of my journey and that I would overcome these irrational thoughts on my own and in my own time. Through his support and patience, he empowered me to be the mum that I am today and in turn enriched my motherhood experience.

As I continued to heal, I realised that I was not alone in my experiences. That other mums had travelled down similar paths to mine and that there will be mums in the future who may also experience a similar journey. Knowing this gave me strength to overcome my insecurities and enabled me to reach out to others for support. It is now my turn to give back the support to others who may experience the same.

3. **I don't know who I am anymore.**
Who am I trying to impress? This was always the question in my head. But in hindsight, I realised that I was trying to impress myself. Nobody expected me to be anyone but myself. I could have relaxed the expectations I placed on myself and still ended up in the same place minus the silver

strands of hair on my head caused by excessive worrying.

I had to remind myself that being a mum is hard work, that I could not do all the things that I had planned to do, and it was okay. The only important things were to love my baby, be present with my baby, play with him, go out for a walk, relax my mind and love the one and only version of me that I saw in the mirror.

The perfect idea of motherhood that I promoted to myself was based on someone else's ideals and not my own. The truth is that motherhood is not a reflection of what you should do or who you should be; a mother is who you become once your baby is born, and therefore every mother is unique and beautiful as her own being.

How I Rediscovered Myself
The road to self-discovery took a lot of motivation and commitment. I focused on my core needs and wants by reflecting on myself, redefining my purpose and upskilling myself to love the person that I am, as I am. I challenged myself with questions that I had deliberately ignored in the past because the thought of asking these questions meant that some form of transformation would have to take place. I focused on having a positive growth mindset and accepted the fact that having to do things differently was a change

that I would either lead or it would be led for me by other external forces. But, ultimately, the transformations needed to happen as part of my evolution, which I knew would deliver a positive impact for myself and my loved ones. I was able to reach a place of balance by mastering the following points:

1. Accepting that I have the power to control my thoughts and my thoughts have the power to control me.
2. Accepting that irrational thoughts were part of my post-partum anxiety and I needed others to help me to overcome this.
3. Accepting that I was not living my authentic self and that I could live my authentic self if I wanted to.
4. Letting go of my fears by giving myself permission to make mistakes and to learn from them.
5. Letting go of my idealised version of motherhood and forgiving myself for not achieving my own targets with regards to this.
6. Letting go of my feelings of failure for not being the mum I thought I would be.

Laila, the Happy Mum

Laila was new to our mothers' group. Her daughter, Nora, was a couple of weeks younger than the other eight-week-old babies in our group.

Laila's family had relocated back to Sydney from Honolulu as her husband pursued a higher role within the multinational company he worked for. As we know, most big roles come with big responsibilities, and this meant that he was often out of town, leaving Laila on her own to care for Nora.

We were getting ready for our daily walk across the bay with our caravan of prams when Laila tripped over some construction debris and scraped her knees. We all quickly put our prams' brakes on to help her get back up on her feet.

As she dusted herself off, she started laughing hysterically. Pulling her hair back from her face, she confessed that she had not slept in days and that she may not have even tripped; perhaps she fell asleep momentarily. There was a roar of laughter from all of us – despite her sleep deprivation, she was still able to have a good sense of humour.

Laila was beautiful. I admired the way she carried herself with dignified poise while being casual at the same time. What stood out the most to me was how relaxed she always appeared to be.

I was intrigued to find out what her secret was to this state of bliss.

We spent a lot of time together – playdates at her home, my home, and at the park. We were together from 8 AM to 5 PM every weekday. I had secretly hoped to be infected by her enthusiasm and relaxed nature as I continued to battle against my own inner turmoil.

Laila told me that she did not have any symptoms of post-partum anxiety. She jokingly said that perhaps it was because she did not read any baby books as she didn't have the attention span to read a book from start to finish. She also said that she did not want to return to work at all, preferring to be a stay-at-home mum.

Meanwhile, I was thinking about re-establishing my career, going back to work, and not being a stay-at-home mum. I realised that I wasn't enjoying being a mum because I was not fully engaged in my present state as my thoughts were consumed by the future.

Laila helped me to be in the present, to relax and enjoy today with my baby. "They grow up so quickly," she would say. She was right.

Laila and I both enjoyed each other's company and we respected each other for our individuality. We appreciated the differences in our parenting styles and we helped each other through the challenging days of caring for our babies.

Some of the values we both agreed on were to have unconditional self-love and to avoid (*where possible*) comparing ourselves to others.

While some comparisons to others are healthy and may increase comradery, when taken to the extreme where the comparison is used as a measure of success or failure, it may result in unrealistic goals and unintended consequences. For example, the meaning of success may be different for each of us. Some may believe that success is achieved when you are living your true self – confident, courageous, loving, and kind. While others may measure success on their access to freedom, to be able to do what they want, whenever they want. What we can all agree on is success is an individual measure and there are many aspects of successful outcomes just as there are of failures.

Laila would sometimes remind me to accept myself and let go of the disappointments. All the baby books in the world will not give you a true indication of what it will be like once the baby joins the family. The reason for this is that everybody's situation is different.

I now know that there are a lot of changes that happen to the body and mind when the baby arrives. While feelings of happiness and love for the new baby are obvious, some mums will also have irrational thoughts, and become lonely and confused. Whenever you feel like it, share your feelings with people you trust. Sometimes, other people may be able to support you to release the negative thoughts and inspire rational thinking. Ultimately, the sooner you are able to regain your self-esteem, the better it will be for both you and your baby.

Food for Thought

All babies can be demanding, and having a baby does not stop you from moving from nursery rooms to boardrooms and back again.

To live a life of confidence begins with loving yourself unconditionally. Self-love is the most powerful love. Without self-love, we are unable to love others in the manner they truly deserve, and once you can do this, you will be ready for the next chapter, which is all about connections.

Chapter 4

Making Connections

"A person is not an island," she said

Some return-to-work mums experience difficulties integrating back into the workplace because of the stigma attached to the responsibilities of motherhood, which may make it appear as though mothers are only capable of limited work output compared to colleagues who are not in the same position.

This stigma is unfair. Return-to-work mums often work harder to prove this idea wrong. Remember, the choice of being a stay-at-home mum or working in a job versus having a career is rarely based only the family circumstances. Rather, it also includes personal considerations based on the wants and needs of the individual. That is, some mums may choose to stay at home, others may continue to invest in their career progression while others simply want to work and get paid for it.

Having a baby and balancing a career at the same time is a rewarding experience. I have two children, six years apart in age, and after both pregnancies, when I returned to work from maternity leave, I moved into more senior roles with more responsibilities. I thrived on the additional opportunities and cherished my moments with my kids, both at the same time.

It's All about Connections

Connections relate to the act of connecting with people and the state of being connected. The first step towards preparing to return to work after maternity leave is to ensure that return-to-work expectations are defined and that supporting connections are strong. This means that while on maternity leave, it is advantageous to plan your return-to-work activities while strengthening your connections to the outside world.

It is so effortless for a new mum to become solely focused on her baby while on maternity leave, that she may inadvertently ignore her other connections in the process. It is important to know that engaging with others and maintaining connections is integral to returning to work.

By the end of this chapter, you will learn how to strengthen your connections during maternity leave and return to work with focus.

Most women I have coached have said that returning to work after having a baby is about satisfying their needs. They know that their baby would most likely prefer to be with them all day rather than for them to be at work. However, the need to be connected to other people, the need to have a higher purpose and the need to achieve their personal goals can be balanced with their motherhood responsibilities, especially when they realise that the time they spend with their baby before and after work can still be an enriching experience for both themselves and their baby.

They also share that the strength of their connections is a critical factor that can predict how successfully they are able to balance motherhood and a satisfying career at the same time.

There are ways to build and maintain connections that produce positive and negative outcomes. Focusing on the positive approaches to human interactions is important to maintaining healthy connections. Similarly, an understanding of what negative connections can be may better prepare mums for the personalities they may encounter when they return to work.

Women who enjoyed their career prior to having a baby will most likely want to continue working at some point in the future. These women do not necessarily change their personal goals, ambitions, and desires after the baby is born. However, there are some who will need to continue working only for financial reasons and are not necessarily returning to work for career satisfaction. This duality does not negate the importance of returning to work as both motivations serve a significant purpose in life.

Whatever the reason for returning to work, women typically have a more difficult time transitioning from the nursery room to the boardroom than men. The reasons for this include but are not limited to: men generally earn higher wages than women (even for comparable jobs), that women are considered to be the primary carers of newborn babies, and high costs or unavailability of suitable childcare options.

Childcare

I was at the tail-end of my job at one of the local companies when my second son was born. I decided to take a year off on maternity leave, and during this time, I planned to turbo-charge my coaching career. I devoted many hours to studying coaching, upskilling myself and coaching clients. Coaching requires uninterrupted attention. Therefore, I knew the importance of ensuring my childcare arrangements were organised prior to launching my practice.

An important decision for me was to enrol my son into the childcare facility across the road from our house because it was known to be the best in the area and conveniently located.

This childcare facility was very popular and only admitted eight babies at a time – it certainly did not have enough room to facilitate the demands from the entire community.

I had enrolled my son into this childcare facility as soon as I found out I was pregnant. During my first call, they informed me that I was on the waiting list and that chances of a successful placement were slim, considering I was at number 645 on the list.

I immediately knew that I needed to work hard on building my connections with this facility in order to secure a placement, as it was the key to my ability to return to work without fuss.

When my baby was born, I arranged a meeting with the Centre Director, and she took me on a tour. She explained that the nursery could only accommodate a maximum of eight babies and that the minimum age was four months old.

In the meantime, we made an effort to become familiar with the childcare workers from the facility, and they got to know us very well. By the time my son turned four months old, we got a call from the Centre Director to offer him a placement for three days a week.

We happily took it, and a few months later, my son was in full-time care with them. He thrived at this centre. His carers were wonderful and we became friends with some of the parents who had their children there too. I believe that this centre contributed to my son's amazing personal development. We have many fond memories of this centre and are still in contact with some of the people who cared for him.

Planning to return to work means having the right childcare in place. This gives you the confidence to focus on work without having to worry about the well-being of your baby.

Without proper childcare facilities in place, returning to work will be difficult and impossible for some. Therefore, it is important that you invest the time in researching the childcare options available to you and use your connections to leverage the best outcome for you and your baby.

I was able to continue coaching during my maternity leave because of the connections I had made to facilitate the care of my baby while I was at work; childcare gave me the opportunity to balance motherhood and career.

How Do You Find the Right Childcare Facility?
The right childcare facility will depend largely on

your needs and expectations. Therefore, it will differ depending on individual circumstances. For return-to-work mums, the most important factor to consider above all is the safety of your baby while in the care of others. You need carers who you can trust with your baby. Without this trust in place, your return to work may not be sustainable. The reason for this is simply that looking after a baby is a full-time job. It requires complete attention, dedicated focus and extreme patience. It is reasonable to expect to have an experienced carer who will give your baby the same level of love and attention that you would, without compromise.

Often, grandparents are the first people to offer childcare assistance. As lovely as this sounds, it does involve planning and setting boundaries in order to avoid miscommunication and relationship fractures.

If there is one relationship that my clients discuss most during this period (other than the relationship shared with their SO), it is the one with their parents or in-laws. This relationship is often tested when different views are presented and sensitivities are ignited, sometimes resulting in extended periods of chaos and drama. However, it is often with clear communication and boundaries that this relationship dynamic can be enriched instead of destroyed. In my experience, babies and their grandparents share a beautiful bond. Therefore, babies deserve to have access to their grandparents and enjoy a loving relationship with them.

If you decide to involve the grandparents or other people with the care of your baby, consider the following:

1. They might have their own way of caring for your baby, which might be completely different to how you would do it. For example, they might have their own routine, which might differ to yours. Be okay with this. Remember that this is an important connection for you and your baby. Therefore, encourage them to be comfortable in their own style of caring for your baby so that they too can develop their unique bond with your baby and care for your baby with confidence.
2. They might try to teach you lessons about how to parent because they want to share their experience with you and their grandchild. I believe that this is a process of knowledge sharing and is not intended to criticise your parenting skills. Rather, the motivation is to share their knowledge with you so that they can support you and your baby. Do not take it personally if they make you feel like they know more than you about looking after your baby. In my experience, I have learned most of what I

needed to know about babies from my mother-in-law. My mother-in-law used to tell me, "You will have your way of doing things. I used to do it this way. So, this is the way I'm going to teach you. There is no right or wrong. Relax; just do whatever feels right for you."

If you decide to go with a childcare facility, keep in mind that not all childcare facilities are created equal. Therefore, choose wisely. Observe and research before you decide to leave your baby in their care.

1. Do not expect the childcare worker to have the same degree of love for your baby as you do or to follow your routine. They will create their own bond with your baby and have their own routine.
2. The quality of the childcare facilities depends on the quality of their childcare workers. Get to know the childcare workers and see how the facility is managed before you commit to entrusting them with your baby's care.
3. Research and analyse their reviews online or from word of mouth. What experiences do other families have with them? What is the turnover rate of their employees? Do they provide all the facilities that you need? For example, some centres provide access to their daily activities through on-site cameras so that you can watch

your baby throughout the day while other centres do not have this available.

Other Connections You Will Need to Return to Work
Once you have determined and secured the appropriate childcare provisions, prepare to invest in strengthening the other connections that will have a significant impact on your return-to-work plans. These are:

Family
Family support is critical for a smooth transition back into the workforce.

When families are supportive of return-to-work mums, the ability to plan and to execute the transition back to the workplace can be easier than for those who lack this support. Family members may offer assistance in caring for the baby, cooking and cleaning. Some mothers may be reluctant to accept offers of assistance while others do not hesitate to welcome the offers. I believe that when returning to work, it is easier to accept assistance from others than to attempt to do everything on your own. The point is to be gracious and welcome any assistance that is offered that will benefit your return to work.

There are some families who are unsupportive of mums returning to work. The reasons for their reservations are wide and personal but are most often due to cultural, belief-based biases or family dynamics. The purpose is not to judge anybody for their life choices; rather, it is to provide support for the women who want to return to work.

Some return-to-work mums will struggle to secure a satisfying career if the family is unsupportive of their decision to return to work. If you are in this situation, there are some steps you can consider that might influence your family to support your return-to-work plans. First of all, discuss your desires to return to work, its benefits, and your plans to overcome the expected challenges. By articulating your plans, you might provide your family with the confidence they need to support your decision to return to work. Ultimately, the decision is yours but the outcome of your decision is not yours alone.

Your boss and team
Keep this connection strong during your maternity leave. It is important if you enjoy feeling included and up-to-date with information.

Maternity leave provides time to continue to demonstrate interest in your team and the company. You can do this by maintaining contact with your colleagues and perhaps even attending work functions, if possible. Be up-to-date with your company performance and your industry. This commitment to your career is going to be evident when you return to work with confidence and clarity.

Your boss will be supportive of your return to work when they understand your return-to-work plans and expectations. Therefore, you need to be clear about these prior to going back to work. For example, if you require specific working hours, flexible arrangements, or anything that differs from your employment agreement, discuss it with your boss before you return to work.

Your boss and your team will welcome you back when you demonstrate that you took the initiative to keep in touch with them during your maternity leave.

There are examples of women returning to work and feeling forgotten and out of the loop.

The way to overcome this is by investing time in rebuilding workplace connections as soon as you return to work. Arrange lunches, coffees and meetings to re-connect with your colleagues.

Share some stories about your time away from work, but do not get offended if colleagues don't show as much interest in your baby as you do. You can also consider demonstrating genuine interest in what the team have been doing and show them how you can contribute to the success of the team and the company by delivering excellent work.

Making Connections

When you return to work from maternity leave, you may have to re-learn new systems and quickly adapt to new ways of doing things. Use your connections to help you to navigate the changed landscape to ensure smooth sailing.

Let me share with you the story of Ivy, who managed to go back to work and thrive because she knew how to positively leverage her connections.

Ivy's Story

Ivy was a thirty-five-year-old corporate lawyer when she was promoted to Group General Counsel. She worked more hours than anyone else in the office and generated high levels of positive returns for the firm. Five years of consistent, hard work resulted in her promotion.

Ivy's husband, Kane, was the Assistant Principal at an exclusive private school. They got married last year and one of their wedding vows was to promise to love and respect each other, no matter what.

Gently fanning a small Polaroid photograph in her slim, porcelain hand, Ivy teasingly told me that she had just had her first scan to confirm that she was pregnant. I was thrilled for her because I knew how much she wanted to have a baby. She said that Kane was so happy that he cried "happy tears" during the ultrasound screening.

Towards the end of her third trimester, with the due date only a few weeks away, Ivy decided that she wanted to return to work forty-five days after giving birth. Their initial plan was for her to return to work after six months, at which time Kane's mum would look after the baby while they were both at work.

However, during her maternity leave, Ivy's company had scaled-up. It was an exciting time for the firm and Ivy wanted to be back at work to drive some of the strategic growth initiatives. Her boss confirmed that he was willing to have her back as soon as she was ready.

Ivy discussed her plans with Kane and asked if he would take time off work instead to look after their baby. She wanted to return to work sooner than they had agreed and planned for. Kane had not expected to take time off work but was supportive of Ivy's decision to return to work.

Kane discussed his plans with his boss, which resulted in Kane working part-time for twelve months. They had also established a routine for both their mums (Ivy's and Kane's) to take turns in caring for their baby until they had secured the childcare placement.

Ivy's story demonstrates the power of strong connections. Therefore, invest the time and effort in building and strengthening all of your positive connections. Especially those who love you and your baby.

In a Nutshell
As the old saying goes, it takes a village to raise a child. Your connections are members of your village so they need to be respected and valued. In return, they can support your return-to-work plans and give you the resources to balance motherhood and your career.

While it is understandable to want to do everything yourself, it wise to be open-minded about opportunities for your connections to add value to your life. Do not be tempted to isolate yourself for long periods of time during maternity leave. Strengthen your connections by maintaining contact with your family, friends, and colleagues, and reserve some time to make new friends.

In the next chapter, we will learn about goal setting for return-to-work mums. The art of goal setting is an important skill in business but it can also be beneficial at home. For example, without goal setting, it can be difficult to define what goals and activities are required in order to achieve a desired target. There is no right or wrong way of doing this, but there are tested methods of creating goals that deliver successful outcomes.

Turn the page, and I will talk more about goal setting for career mums – how do you create and measure them? What do you do with them? Are you ready?

Chapter 5

Golden Goals for Golden Girls

90% Planning and 10% Doing

It has been said that living a life of fulfilment means living a life that is desired, promised or predicted. Therefore, it is wise to create life goals and objectives. There are some life events that we can prepare for more than others. For example, a wedding party can be a beautiful event to organise. The timeframes are pre-defined, the budgets forecasted and the outcome is clear – the happy couple say "I do" and hold hands into their future of togetherness. On the other hand, we know that babies do not come with an instruction manual. Once a baby is born, mums are pushed into their new life of motherhood. As for working mums, they are required to balance caring for the baby, caring for themselves, investing time towards their career, and being available for their family and everyone else around them. To these mums, the world may appear to be chaotic.

Goals are designed to articulate visions and desires that ultimately translate into meaningful plans of action. Life goals might include self-love, family and career. To create these goals, you will need a road map to plan and activate your vision.

If you are currently on maternity leave, think about your career-centric goals and visualise your plans for the future. You have the power to strategically align your life goals with your career goals and build the framework that will help you to achieve both of these in harmony. In this chapter, you will learn about the importance of setting goals and why we need them.

As humans, we live in a world where goals are established for us from an early age. For example, at school, we are required to learn and to demonstrate understanding. As a result, a grade is awarded for our level of understanding and competence. We use these basic rules in business, when we get paid for the type of work that we produce as dictated by the business.

Mum and baby goals are often set by the paediatrician. The aim is to ensure a healthy baby by achieving specific developmental milestones within the pre-defined timeframes. During this period, these are the most important goals to be achieved by mum and baby.

For return-to-work mums, this can also be the time to reconfigure career goals. Try not to get stuck with the excuse that it's all about the baby and not about the mum because this is simply unrealistic.

The first few months with a baby will most likely be a tiring experience. Confusion, nervousness and sometimes even disappointments may surface. For example, at times when expectations are not met and your SO does not seem to do as much as you think he should be doing.

The personal goals that mums try to achieve during these first few months are: to make sure the baby is healthy, to feel rested, to keep the house tidy, to eat and to maintain a healthy hygiene standard.

Just as self-love and connections are important, so too is taking the time to set life goals.

The idea of goal setting may seem basic. The hard part is believing in the power of goal setting and then activating this power to create goals for yourself that transform your desires into reality.

What Is a Goal?

A goal can be explained as the object of a person's ambition or the effort invested by a person for a desired result.

In the workplace, goals are necessary. They align the

output of our role with the desired outcome of the business. In return for this service, we earn a salary and secure our job.

Goal setting is the vehicle to turn our visions into reality, and we know that a vision that can't be translated into reality is only ever going to remain a dream.

If you want to bring your dreams to life, you need to have goals. Goals are the first step to every journey. Without goals, does it really matter which direction you take?

Just imagine, you plan to return to work but still have not made childcare arrangements. You would feel rather disappointed if you were unable to secure childcare and your work was given to someone else because of your inability to return to work on time. By planning and using your connections, a different outcome may have been presented.

Or perhaps you have secured childcare and returned to work but did not plan your new working conditions and required hours of work. You would feel disappointed if you were unable to complete your tasks on time and this situation may result in a lack of attention to other areas in your life.

These are some examples and perhaps there are other examples that are more relevant to you. The point is, setting goals can be a rewarding experience once you are able to achieve them.

It is important that you have the motivation to set your goals. There is no perfect formula for goal setting; you have the freedom to choose whatever structure works for you.

The Need for Goal Setting

Below are some more practical reasons for goal setting:

1. To strategically plan for life goals and define the required resources and corresponding activities.
2. To focus attention onto areas that will deliver profitable results and avoid areas that will deplete time and energy (it is important to identify areas of benefit and minimise non-beneficial activities).
3. To measure progress and motivate progression towards the end goal.
4. To encourage commitment, discipline and to avoid procrastination.

There are countless articles and learning resources available to increase your goal-setting skills. In my experience, the hardest part of goal setting is starting the goal-setting process.

Once you've decided to start goal setting, invest in the time that it will take to do it. Consider visualising your future with some of the following questions:

1. What are your goals?
2. What do you want to achieve?
3. How will your goals impact your life and the lives of those around you?
4. What will the future be like once you've achieved your goals?

Set the Goals That Motivate You
Be authentic to what it is you really want. For example, while you are on maternity leave, you might set goals to become the Chief Executive Officer. You may consider this goal as either short-, medium- or long-term, the difference being the timeframe that you set yourself to achieve the goals.

Short-term goals: Daily, weekly, monthly, quarterly.

Medium-term goals: Might align with short-term goals. Can be achieved and measured over one to five years.

Long-term goals: Might align with medium-term goals. Can be achieved and measured over five years and beyond.

You might consider the following points to include

in your goal setting to becoming a Chief Executive Officer:

1. Childcare: short-term.
2. Return-to-work plans: short- to medium-term.
3. Position-specific education and training: medium- to long-term.
4. Relationship with connections: short-, medium- and long-term.

Whatever your current circumstances may be, you need to be passionate about your goals, and your goals need to be authentic and achievable in the time that you are at in your life. There is no point in setting a goal that you are not passionate about or setting a goal to please others around you and not yourself. Make your goals SMARTER.

SMARTER goals are:

Specific
- What exactly do you want from this goal?
- Is anyone else involved?
- What are the challenges?
- How will you achieve this?

Measurable
- What is the timeframe to achieve this?
- How do you know when you've achieved this?

Achievable
- Is this goal realistic?

Relevant
- What is the reason for this goal?
- Is this goal worthwhile?

Time-bound
- What is the deadline for this goal?
- Is there a timeline?
- Can you achieve this goal in six months?

Evaluate
Continuously evaluate your goals and your progress, as this can help you to stay focused and motivated.

Readjust
Goals are created to be adjusted. This means that you should not get stuck in continuing to pursue a goal that will not complement you. Similarly, do not continue to pursue a goal with no purpose. You have the power to readjust your goals.

Let us do an exercise. Here is a table where you can plan your SMARTER goals and understand what you really want to do. Enter your goals in the table below. The more you use goal-setting methods, the better you'll become at it.

Focus	Goal 1	Goal 2	Goal 3
Specific			
Measurable			
Achievable			
Relevant			
Time Bound			
Evaluate			
Readjust			

This table works for me. However, there are plenty of other goal-setting templates available. Use whichever template works for you. These templates serve as a record of your goals and can lead to increased motivation and commitment.

The Story of Emily

I have coached a few clients who have gone through divorce and one thing that they commonly share with me is how disappointed they are because they did not achieve their goal of having the perfect family life.

In my experience, when I coach women who are going through, or have recently gone through, a divorce, their divorce stories have a similar theme of feelings of shame and failure. It is only when we accept the truth – that shame is a self-inflicted feeling, failure is a temporary experience and there is no such thing as a perfect family – that we can outgrow these feelings and evolve into a powerful person.

Emily was forty-five years old, and a recently divorced, single mum of two, who discovered that her husband of eighteen years had been keeping busy at work with more than just his spreadsheets. Needless to say, Emily felt abandoned, angry and betrayed.

Shared custody of the children, a twelve-year-old and a fifteen-year-old, gave Emily time to rediscover herself after years of being a stay-at-home mum and caring for others first before herself.

Emily said that she and her ex-husband hadn't been intimate or affectionate towards each other for many years prior to the divorce.

The divorce energised Emily to look after herself and focus on her wants and needs.

Emily's primary goal was to reclaim her life and

be the person that she wanted to be. She did not recognise the Emily that was staring back at her in the mirror.

Her other goals were to lose weight, take pride in her appearance, go back to work and meet a new man while continuing to be the awesome mum that she is.

For each kilogram she shed, she gained more energy. She booked appointments with her hairdresser, got her nails done, made new connections and started dating again. Eventually, she settled down with her new man, her former childhood sweetheart, who was also divorced.

Now, you might think that Emily could have achieved all of this without setting goals. Perhaps she could have. However, she said that soon after her divorce, she struggled to motivate herself to do anything worthwhile and could not focus long enough to think about anything beyond what would happen in the next five minutes. She became depressed and lonely. Then, one day, she sat at the laptop and started typing a letter to herself.

In this letter, she wrote what she had hoped for her future self and, as a result, helped her current self to generate ideas on what to do to get her to where she wanted to be in her life (goals).

She printed out the letter, left it under her pillow overnight and slept on it. The next day, she read it with her morning coffee and was immediately energised into action. These were her goals and she set a timeline to achieve them.

The last time I saw Emily, I asked her if there were any goals she was still working on. She replied that she wanted to bump into her ex-husband to show off her new man and her revenge body.

In Essence

Some believe that life does not just happen to you. You can make life happen when you design goals that are right for you. Goals can transform what is in your imagination into reality because they can help to define what you need to have in place in order to bring your dreams to life.

In addition, goal setting is an important tool to drive focus and motivation. The absence of clear goals can result in decreased opportunities and unidentified risks that can block progress. I use goal setting to manage the areas of my life that I can control. I prefer to be the driver of my life rather than the passenger.

I hope this chapter motivates you to define your goals and to commit to achieving them. In the next chapter, I will share some traits of good people and some traits of toxic people. We know that everyone is different and this difference results in people who will be good for us and those who will be toxic.

Do you want to know more? Let's turn the page.

Chapter 6

Good and Toxic

We are all unique, just like everybody else

The world is made up of different people. People have different shapes and sizes, different wants and needs, different ambitions and beliefs. Therefore, it is natural to expect there will be people who are good for us and those who are toxic for us, and those that are in between, sometimes good, sometimes toxic.

In my experience, people gravitate towards people who make them feel good. We know when people make us feel good because they elevate our spirits, support us in our time of need, encourage us to bring our goals to life and influence us to make better decisions. Toxic people have the opposite effect. However, this is not as prescriptive as good versus toxic because there are people who appear to be good for us, but when we examine the impact that they have on our lives by reflecting with questions such as, "What role have they played in supporting my goals?" or, "Do their values align with mine?", the answers may be surprising.

On the other hand, there are people who appear toxic but might be good for us because their different perspectives might influence us to transform into the person that we want to be.

The aim here is to identify the difference between these two opposites and to apply your knowledge to attract the people who will support your goals and celebrate your success and avoid those who will distract you from achieving your desired goals.

Toxic people are ubiquitous and, truth be told, you, too, could be toxic for someone else.

A friend of mine once told me that there are toxic traits in all of us, and when we accept this, we can better manage these traits within ourselves and identify them in others. This is the required level of self-awareness that gives us the ability to expertly guide situations at home and at work.

By the end of this chapter, you will be able to identify the top personality traits of good and toxic people and how you can maximise your social interactions at home and at work.

Understanding People

Mums returning to work will need the support of reliable colleagues to help them to navigate their return-to-work process, and as we have already mentioned, return-to-work mums need support from as many people (connections) as possible.

When working with people, we are exposed to many different emotions. We can never really know exactly what a person is thinking, and it's not our role to guess either.

Understanding people, managing emotions and mastering social interactions are some of the ingredients to being a good connector, and good connectors have an advantage over those who are not, as people will tend to be more supportive of those they choose to "like" compared to those they "don't like".

Therefore, having a good understanding of people and how to engage others can lead to a more successful transition for working mums.

Identifying Toxicity

One day, I was at my office when a colleague asked if she could come in and see me. We didn't have a scheduled meeting. However, since I had time before my next meeting, I welcomed her in to have a chat.

She asked me, "Have you accidentally listened in on

a conversation while minding your own business in the office toilet cubicle?"

I said, "No, not yet."

Before I could ask her anything else, she asked, "If you did, would you make a sound to let them know that you were there or would you remain quiet so that you don't interrupt them?"

I was not sure where the conversation was heading so I asked her if I could assist her with anything. She said she wanted to tell me a story, and here it goes.

Earlier that day, she was in the ladies' room when she heard two familiar voices outside by the sink, heavily engaged in conversation. She was locked inside her cubicle, and they were oblivious to the risk that there could have been someone else listening to what they were saying.

She said they were talking about Sally, one of our colleagues, whose promotion to General Manager had been announced a few hours earlier. She said that Sally's friends, Gemma and Christine, were talking about Sally in a very negative way.

You see, Gemma and Christine were Sally's friends. The three of them were known as the tri-stars of the company; they were together most lunchtimes and some weekends too. Over the few years of working together, these three women had become good friends in and out of the office.

She said it surprised her to hear that both Gemma and Christine thought that the only reason Sally got the promotion was that her skirt was shorter than theirs and that she didn't have the capability to perform the role that she had been promoted to. But what made her feel uncomfortable was what they were planning to do to Sally. She said they were going to ignore Sally at work. They would stop inviting Sally to lunch and then wait to see how long it would take for Sally to realise that they did not want to be her friend anymore.

She asked me what she should do with this information. I told her that, in my experience, it is best to keep a distance from unprofessional behaviour and maintain discretion, especially since the topic of conversation she had listened in on was not business-related.

I have been in business long enough to say with confidence that there will be toxic people, just like Gemma and Christine, at every company. This is a fact, and the sooner we accept it, the more control we have over how we respond. Some colleagues can be insecure; they can gossip and disengage team members. Then there are those good colleagues who will support you and inspire you to perform your best.

In addition to this, you might have an expectation that all family members are good. This is incorrect! Toxic people exist everywhere, and family members are no exception. However, the difference is that we tend to forgive family members and accept their faults, no matter how detrimental this may be to our own well-being.

For example, the toxic person could be the brother who constantly parades his opinions about your baby either being too skinny because you are not feeding your baby enough food or perhaps your baby is overweight because of your poor nutritional choices. Or it could be the sister who compares her more intelligent children to your baby and insinuates that this is because she spends more time with her children than you do with yours, and therefore you should follow her example and raise your baby as she does if you want your baby to be clever and happy like hers. If these judgements and opinions have a negative impact on your self-esteem and well-being, they can be considered toxic.

It is easier to identify toxic people in your family and friendship groups than colleagues at work. The reason for this is that, with family and friends, we have the advantage of being able to know their personalities and we have the advantage of distancing ourselves whenever we want to. Whereas at work, some colleagues will not share their complete persona, preferring to remain guarded. Also, it is more complicated to deliberately distance ourselves from colleagues as the expectation is that we work together.

Top Toxic Traits in Workplace
Here are some examples of toxic traits and how to manage them:

1. **The Gossip**
   This person is detrimental for teams. They can harm the work culture by preventing solutions and innovation, strain relationships and decrease productivity. An old saying is "Be careful who you trust. If someone can openly discuss other people with you, they will certainly discuss you with others."

   To be clear, the gossip spreads rumours, shares false information, speaks negatively and humiliates others, leaks confidential information and continues these behaviours even when encouraged to stop.

   The gossip is usually insecure and is in desperate need of attention. Their stories are their currency, and what they want is for you to listen to them because they think that their stories can be exchanged for camaraderie between the two of you and to decrease the credibility of the person they are gossiping about. Generally, this person is unhappy about their current situation at work or perhaps even in life.

Gossip is their means of connecting with you, usually to incite more gossip, which may be used against you in the future.

On the positive side, most teams know who the gossip is and they are generally not highly respected in the workplace, despite what the gossip may tell you.

To protect yourself from this character, you simply need to keep your interactions at a professional level. Do not participate in the gossip by adding unnecessary information to the conversation, divert the topic away from the gossip, stay focused and focus on solutions at all times.

The only cure for gossip is to say nothing.

2. **The Drama**

    This person lacks the self-awareness required to be professional in business because they confuse the workplace with their theatrical stage. They will almost always have a crisis story and will exaggerate their role in any given situation. The fuel for the drama is more drama.

    The drama can ignite conflict, defer innovation and erode trust.

In my experience, this character usually does not understand what's going on in their own head. They don't know how to properly manage their emotions at work.

Identifying these traits in others is easy, particularly if you happen to be at the receiving end of their bad mood. The first rule is not to take it personally. Their behaviour is owned by them, and you do not have to buy it. However, if you feel it is necessary, you could calm them down by asking them what is going on that is making them behave in this way. This often leads to some self-reflection. However, be prepared to accept that these dramatic personalities are beyond your help.

The best thing to do in these situations is to keep calm. Do not buy into their drama, and when the dust settles, ask them how they are feeling.

The drama will suck the life out of you if you allow it. Protect yourself from the drama by focusing on your work and your performance. Keep the smile on your face despite their sour looks.

3. **The Victim**

    This person is easy to sympathise with in the beginning. You may even feel sorry for them and buy into their sufferings. However, as time passes, you realise that despite all your one-on-ones, no progress is being made because they continually feel sorry for themselves and complain a lot more than others.

The victim cannot be helped by others to get out of the victim mindset; they are the only ones who can help themselves out of it.

This toxic character can damage team morale and company culture. They can also waste the valuable time and resources of others with their victim stories, leaving very little time to focus on productive goals. The victim is skilled at dividing teams and souring relationships at work, so it is best to leave the victim to focus on their own issues.

When you realise that your colleague has been taking up a lot of your time on their issues, which they don't seem to address themselves, help them to reach a level of self-awareness by re-focusing their thinking on solutions instead of just problems. You can do this by asking them questions about, "Have you considered doing it another way?" or, "Have you tried changing whatever it is that is bothering you?"

The victim is good at finding an audience that will listen to them. Return-to-work mums are a prime target for this character because the return-to-work mum will most likely welcome interactions with all colleagues; she also seeks information and wants to feel included. Just remember to keep your relationship professional and do not fall into the trap of commenting on the victim stories.

4. **The Jealous**

   Jealousy is the outcome of many negative emotions such as anger, frustration, hurt and envy. Jealousy in the workplace most often comes from insecurity, especially evident when the jealous person needs to put others down in order to make themselves feel better.

There may be colleagues who will be jealous of you, and you cannot ignore that fact. For example, if you are the return-to-work mum with a cute baby, exuding confidence and a career that's been waiting for you while you sipped lattes at the park with your mothers' group, you may attract the attention of the jealous person, especially when your outstanding performance at work is gaining recognition from others.

To protect yourself from this character, do not entertain their negative gossiping about others. You could also ask them why they feel this way about another colleague.

Ultimately, the best thing to do is to continue to keep a professional relationship, with a distance. Where possible, recognise their achievements to boost their self-esteem – a little compliment may go a long way towards alleviating their negative emotions.

5. **The Narcissist**
   The narcissist or the self-absorbed person will make you feel alone when you are with them. Their topic of discussion will be whatever they choose it to be, and you are just the audience in their presence.

   They appear confident and, given the opportunity, will tell you stories that they feel are important (usually about themselves) and will exaggerate their capabilities. They will conveniently "forget" to tell you about the latest data that you need to feed into your strategic plan that you needed to present to the board.

   These people are not team players and will not perform well in leadership roles as they have their own agenda and teamwork is not on it.

   The best plan of action here is to keep this relationship cordial. Avoid trying to build a strong bond in the hope that this person will change. They will not change unless they want to and you are not going to affect that.

   These are the top five toxic traits to be aware of at work. Be mindful that you, too, might demonstrate some of these behaviours, and if you do, reflect on what has caused you to behave in this way so that you manage your presence and personal brand in the future.

Top Good Traits at Work

You have learnt how to identify and deal with different kinds of toxic people at work. Now here are the good traits that you need to look for:

1. **The Self-aware**

    This person knows themselves and the impact of their actions and behaviours on others. Whether their intention is to be firm but fair, or soft and easy-going, they know how to use their modalities to get the message clearly across to others and avoid confusion.

    Often described as professional and authentic, people with high degrees of self-awareness know how to behave and how to inspire trust and confidence in others.

2. **The Respectable**

    This person knows that they are not better than anyone else and demonstrates respect for others. Their word and their way of thinking are precious and valued. This person makes people feel valued.

A respectable person is known for professionalism and courage. They behave in the right manner and inspire others to behave in the same way.

3. **The Intelligent**
   Intelligent people tend to focus on intelligent outcomes and avoid traits that toxic people demonstrate.

   Here, intelligence is defined as the ability to acquire and apply knowledge and skills. It is easy to spot the intelligent person at work; they are usually the ones who do not participate in gossip and drama. Instead, they have gravitas and attract other colleagues to use them as mentors.

   Align yourself with intelligent people because they can provide the springboard to your continued success and satisfaction.

4. **The Diligent**
   This person is easy to spot because they work hard and rarely subscribe to the pettiness that surrounds them brought on by toxic people.

   The diligent person can either be a quiet achiever or a promoter. Either way, they will get the job done without fuss or drama.

   Align yourself with a diligent person because they have the power to motivate you to continue to work towards your goals and to eventually achieve them.

5. The Empath
This person is the one that others talk about in a positive manner. You will often hear that so-and-so person is kind. You will feel better being around this person because they know how you feel and can be a mirror for your thoughts and emotions.

This person will listen to you and never judge you or give you unwanted advice. Listening is their strength.

People want to be with people who make them feel good and add value to their lives.

If you identify someone in your life with these five traits, hold on to them because they can support you in achieving your goals. It's also important to work on improving these traits in yourself so that you are not a toxic person in someone else's life.

The Story of Sally

When you have the knowledge to understand the differences between good people and toxic people, you are better able to protect yourself from the behaviours of others and rise above every situation.

Sally noticed that since she got her promotion, her good friends Gemma and Christine were organising lunches without her. Having worked together in the same team for over two years, the ladies had developed a strong bond of friendship inside and outside of work.

It was a surprising and sudden change for Sally when both Gemma and Christine excluded her from intra-office chats.

It was obvious to Sally that she was being excluded, and this made her feel alienated and insecure.

When Sally came in to see me, she told me that she did not know how to handle the current situation with her friends, and that she had not expected them to alienate her when she was promoted and became their boss.

Instead of focusing her attention on trying to salvage the relationships, Sally decided to focus on the behaviours that got her the promotion in the first place – her good traits.

She dusted herself off and walked out of my office with her head held high.

She organised a meeting with Gemma and Christine and outlined her expectations of them. She did not address her feelings of lost friendship, instead focusing on being professional.

Within six months, Gemma left to join another company. Sally and Christine, on the other hand, continued working together until Sally was promoted into an even more senior role, leaving Christine in the same position. Christine now has a new boss, who was also a peer of hers, promoted into a role that Christine had also interviewed for.

Toxic people exist in any business. It is our goal to rise above them so that we can all continue to enjoy working in a company with a strong culture. When you surround yourself with toxic people, you will be toxic too. Be professional and polite but try to distance yourself from them.

The same rule applies to toxic family members. Distance yourself from all the toxicity so that you can achieve the goals that you have set for yourself. Find positive influencers instead. They are easy to spot and will welcome those who are not toxic. You can support each other for successful outcomes.

Life is a marathon where toxic people will eventually run out of fuel to succeed in the long run.

People who demonstrate good traits will always be valued, wherever they go.

Let's Reflect on this Topic

In this world, there are good people and there are toxic people. You will encounter both at home and at work. The aim is to be able to identify them and know what to do when they are in your life and you are in theirs.

You are in control of who you choose to surround yourself with. You have the power to attract or detract people from your space.

Therefore, be a master of self-awareness. You can measure your mastery by knowing who you are and what impact you have on others. Ask yourself, "Am I a good person or am I toxic?" In accepting the fact that the difference between good and toxic depends on individual situations and what role people play in your life, you will overcome disappointments brought on by others when they do not meet your expectations of them.

Let us now move on to the next chapter, where we talk about celebrating success and learning from failures.

Learning to celebrate success in a timely manner and in a way that feels deserved is one of the key skills required to live a life of fulfilment.

Some say that it is not easy for a woman to feel successful and often the confidence that comes with success is overshadowed by her desire to overlook her achievements in order to move on to the next goal, so as not to attract attention to herself.

Instead, take time to reflect on your achievements. Promote your achievements to others before moving on to your next goals because self-promotion is not a sin. It is a powerful tool to build confidence and strengthen the foundations of success.

Read further to learn how others have done this.

Chapter 7

The Rise of the Guilt-Free Mummy

Rise, Mummy, Rise

As a Coach, it is my job to partner with my client in a thought-provoking and thoughtful process to allow my client space to reflect on their situation in order to implement the actions and achieve their desired outcomes. It is never about telling clients what to do or how to feel.

One of the most challenging experiences to understand and to overcome for new mums is how to consolidate their feelings of guilt. For example, guilt for returning to work, guilt for leaving their baby in childcare, guilt for being unavailable for the needs of their SO, guilt for not paying the bills on time, guilt for being less than perfect, and so on and so forth.

The reality is, for many return-to-work mums, their minds are consumed by guilty feelings, which can be triggered by anyone or any event – this is called "mummy guilt".

The adjustment from being a full-time mum to a return-to-work mum takes time and resilience. In an ideal world, companies would provide return-to-work mums with a structured reboarding program that could address these issues. As of today, I do not know of any company that has implemented a satisfactory reboarding program for return-to-work mums. Currently, it is acceptable for return-to-work mums to have to navigate the workplace on their own. This can result in deeper feelings of guilt and loneliness.

Basically, the return-to-work mum wraps herself up in her own emotions, silently and diligently getting on with the job, not even realising that she deserves much more support to adjust to her new work environment and lifestyle.

While some organisations have advanced to provide maternity-leave provisions, by and large, the return-to-work provisions still fall short of what is needed. Considering that the percentage of women in the workplace continues to rise, it is time that we improve these provisions in order to attract mums back to the workplace and retain them for the long-term.

Re-entering the workforce from maternity leave is difficult because, although most mums will not admit it, they often struggle with their decision to return to work. "Is it really the right time for me to return to work and be away from my baby?" "Am I doing the right thing?" "Why do I put my own needs over those of my baby?" These are some of the internal questions that haunt return-to-work mums.

What if there is no such thing as the right or wrong time to return to work? All families are different and have different needs and wants. Therefore, there is an endless number of reasons for women to return to work and some of their decisions are not made entirely by their own choice.

What is constant is the underlying guilt and how these guilty feelings can sometimes increase when returning to work.

It is important to overpower this guilt. Otherwise, you will wrap yourself in your own cloth, unable to move or be moved; you will be paralysed for no reason at all.

This chapter will provide you with the tools to unwrap yourself from the emotional constraints of returning to work and tell you how to apply these tools to make guilt-free decisions.

Can You Imagine Doubting Each Decision You Make?

When you are unsatisfied with whatever action you take because you think that the results might make you feel guilty, then you constantly feel uncertain; you believe that you are falling short of expectations all the time. This is mummy guilt. It is real, and if left unexposed, it can erode self-love and confidence.

For example, mums who chose to stay at home after having a baby may feel guilty about not being able to financially contribute towards the household and, at the same time, feel guilty about wanting to return to work. They have put themselves in a *zugzwang*. A *zugzwang* is a situation in the game of chess in which the obligation to make a move in one's turn is a serious, often decisive, disadvantage.

I will expose mummy guilt to clear the path for all mums to rise above it with confidence.

Mum Guilt

Mum guilt is an umbrella of emotions like guilt, doubt, anxiousness or worry. These emotions are experienced by mothers when they worry that they are falling short of expectations in some way.

One of the physicians told me, although mum guilt is not a psychological diagnosis (*yet*), the feelings that accompany it may lead to anxiety and depression if ignored.

Mum guilt is that voice that tells you that you are not a good enough mum, that if you spend one second away from your baby, you are selfish, that if you miss your baby's first bath, your baby will not love you.

These statements are clearly nonsense. If they creep into your thoughts, **do not believe them**. Instead, focus on all the things that you do well and have achieved that make you a great mum. If your feelings of guilt continue, speak to someone about them; share your feelings. Other mums are a great source of support in times like these because they, too, may have experienced mum guilt.

Your baby loves you no matter what. Love and take care of yourself because it's the only self you've got.

Debunking Mum Guilt

Let me share what mum guilt sounds like and how to deal with it.

1. **I feel guilty for hating my pregnancy.**
   You are pregnant, congratulations. However, your uncontrollable nausea and the gagging and dry retching reaction to the smell of lavender render you unfit to go outside.

Understand that not everyone is blessed with a pregnancy glow and luxurious locks. It is perfectly acceptable to not enjoy pregnancy.

2. **I feel guilty for not spending enough time with my baby.**
   Whether it is your need to go to the toilet, take a shower, get your nails done, or return to work, mum guilt will make you feel like you are a bad mum because you've done something for yourself.

   In my opinion, it is perfectly healthy for you to have some time for yourself, away from your baby. Your baby needs to learn to spend some time away from you too. How much time you spend away from each other is completely up to you, and whatever that time is, know that it is okay. There is no right or wrong.

3. **I feel guilty for not enjoying the newborn phase.**
   Newborns are not enjoyable for everyone. This phase only lasts for a short period of time. Eventually, babies will fit into your routine, and you will get to know their routine, making it easier to pre-empt their needs and plan around yours.

   If you feel overwhelmed, talk to someone about it or allow others to care for your baby while you have a break.

4. **I feel guilty for raising my voice.**
   It is natural to get annoyed, and if the way you demonstrate annoyance is to raise your voice, that's okay, too. Your children will not grow up to be less than perfect because you raised your voice on the odd occasion. However, please note that children will imitate the behaviours of those around them who have a strong impact (whether positive or negative).

5. **I feel guilty for not wanting to be intimate with my SO.**
   It is up to you to decide when you are ready for intimacy again. Take your time and focus on self-love first before you prioritise other people's needs and wants. Intimacy is not a race to the finish; it's an evolution of a person, and anything that's worth it, takes time to develop.

6. **I feel guilty for returning to work.**
   It is your decision to return to work. You can focus on the opportunities that your return to work will generate. Returning to work requires constant dedication and effort, both at home and in the workplace. For the first few months of being a career mum, you will be exhausted, but if you enjoy your career, this might motivate you to continue to produce your desired outcomes.

7. **I feel guilty for staying at home.**
   Whether or not it is your choice to stay at home, you are doing it for you and your baby. Determine what it is about staying at home that makes you feel guilty. Is it that you feel like you should contribute more financially towards your household expenses, or do you feel guilty because your SO has such a stressful job and doesn't have the quality time with your baby that you do, or both? Focus on the privileges that you have and enjoy them because time flies quickly.

   If you can, busy yourself with things that you enjoy doing. Get your SO involved with the baby whenever you can.

8. **I feel guilty that my marriage is unstable since the baby arrived.**
   If your marriage is falling apart after your baby is born, I feel sorry to say that it was most likely on the rocks before your baby was born.

   Speak to a trusted friend or seek assistance from a counsellor to help you and your spouse navigate this stressful time.

   Babies require a lot of undivided attention, and this can cause friction for a couple who are adjusting to taking care of a demanding new member in the house.

9. **I feel guilty for not having enough to give my baby.**
   Whatever the perceived lack is, in my experience, your baby does not feel the same way. Focus on what you have and all the love that you give your baby. This is all the baby needs.

When mum-guilt thoughts enter your mind, it will make you feel insignificant and out of control. These thoughts are placed in your own head, by you, so you have the power to get wrapped up in them or uncover them for what they are – just thoughts, devoid of action and powerless to come to life without your permission.

Social media has pushed us to compare ourselves to each other, to live a life that is inauthentic because of the perceived desirability of the lives of those we compare ourselves to. The remedy for this is to focus on being the mum that you are. Sure, you may not be like Betty from the mums' group, who seems to have it all, but you are you, and you are perfect.

Rise above the mum guilt. Practise not comparing yourself to others. Believe that you are perfect just as you are, and then you can enjoy the guilt-free lifestyle that you deserve.

In 2020, I worked at a hospital and continued to do pro-bono coaching during the weekend. I did this and made time to be with my amazing sons. I never felt guilty for balancing work commitments, coaching, and playing with my kids because I knew that by being happy, I was making them happy.

In December 2019, the world reacted to the unexpected arrival of SARS COVID-19, also known as the coronavirus. This deadly virus spread quickly around the world, killing over one million people in six months.

The rapid rate of infection and death toll forced many governments to close their borders and recommend that people quarantine indoors; globally, nations' responses to virus containment were varied. Some countries imposed strict quarantine rules where citizens and residents were not allowed to go outside without wearing a face mask and gloves for fear of transmitting the virus, while other countries were more relaxed.

I was living in Dubai during the COVID-19 outbreak, and at the beginning of 2020, schools, workplaces, tourist hot spots and places of worship were closed to the public. I even had to have a permit in order to go to work as only essential workers were allowed outside their homes.

On a global scale, events such as the 2020 Tokyo Olympics and the 2020 Dubai World Expo were postponed.

The social distancing rule of being two metres apart was encouraged for everyone. This has never before been practised by humans on a global scale. The words "isolation" and "quarantine" became part of our daily lexicon and it was during this period that I coached many mums online through virtual meeting rooms.

A number of mums in isolation were in a dark emotional place brought on by isolation and loneliness. Added to this was the fear of contracting the virus or, worse still, dying from it.

Mums in Isolation

I want to tell you the story of Edith, a client who was quarantined during the SARS COVID-19 pandemic.

Edith was living in Milan, Italy, during the COVID-19 pandemic. She was confined in isolation, in a two-bedroom apartment on the sixth floor, with her husband, Beau, and her eighteen-month-old twin girls, Winnie and Yula.

Edith organised a call with me because she was starved of adult interaction. On our first meeting, she asked why I did not have a glass of wine with me. I told her it was 9 AM in Dubai. We had a laugh, as she held up her bottle of wine.

It had been three weeks since their isolation began. They were quarantined at home, unable to feel the sunshine on their faces or walk the streets. They were only allowed to go to the shops for essential groceries and even then, only one person per household could leave the house.

Edith and Beau would take turns walking their apartment hallway for some alone time from all the chaos at home with the twins. Both of them had been assigned to work from home and as childcare facilities were closed, the girls were with them all day, every day.

This was their life during isolation. Although none of them had the virus, they all had to stay home in order to comply with government isolation orders.

Edith told me that to save herself from going certifiably insane, she started a journal about her life in isolation. She discovered that all of her previous demands on herself to be the perfect mum had disappeared because being locked in the house with her family taught her not to fuss about the little things. She accepted that she will make mistakes and she's okay with it.

During our conversation, Winnie bumped her head on the corner of the coffee table and a bruise immediately popped up. Winnie cried and Edith excused herself from the call to tend to Winnie. I observed that Edith was calm and gentle and Winnie stopped crying as soon as a small bag of frozen vegetables was placed directly on her head.

When Edith returned to our meeting, she said that in the past, she would have been incredibly upset with herself; she would have felt guilty for not preventing the accident. But now, she chooses to not give herself a hard time over these sorts of minor events.

I praised her for the no-worries approach that she had adopted, an approach that clearly made her feel more relaxed and in control.

She also told me that the other day, Yula hit Winnie with the remote control. She raised her voice at Yula but did not feel like a bad mum for this. She needed to demonstrate that she would discipline the girls the way that she wanted to and if this involved raising her voice, then she was okay with that.

Edith told me that since experiencing home isolation, she has so much respect for stay-at-home mums. She said that, for her, staying at home with the kids twenty-four hours a day, seven days a week was a nightmare to begin with. However, over time, she had learnt to enjoy it because she stopped putting pressure on herself to be the perfect mum.

As our call neared its end, Edith said she could not wait for the lockdown to be lifted so that she could return to work again.

It is important to know that all mums experience some degree of mum guilt, and no mum is immune to it. This guilt is self-imposed and only the individual has the power to create it and destroy it.

While we can support the mums who have mum guilt, the key to obliterating it is in shifting the mindset towards acceptance, self-love and positive growth.

Ways to banish mum guilt include:

1. Accepting that it exists and that it can be destroyed by trusting your decisions and subsequent actions.
2. Speaking to someone you trust to vent and let all the feelings out. You will find that doing this may help you to crystallise the fact that your guilt cannot be activated without your permission.
3. Finally, if you are feeling overwhelmed, seek professional advice from your local health nurse or physician.

You have the power to choose to live as a paralysed mummy or a guilt-free mummy.

To Sum it Up
Return-to-work mums might have a difficult time integrating back to work from maternity leave if they have not properly prepared for the changes in their life.

The Rise of the Guilt-Free Mummy

Mum guilt is real and it can be debilitating. If ignored, it leaves the mum in a state of mind-numbing uncertainty. It erodes confidence and self-love. It can stop a return-to-work mum from enjoying life. There are ways to end the mum guilt; the process begins with self-awareness.

You have the power to defeat mum guilt because you know what to do when it starts to creep up on you. By knowing this, you will be able to help yourself through it. You will also be able to help others who may call on you to help them navigate the road ahead to avoid guilt trips.

Now that you have learnt to overpower mum guilt, let's move on to the next chapter where we discuss changes, what it means to be a new mum, and how to adapt to motherhood while having a happy and healthy mind and soul.

Chapter 8

Cha-Cha Changes

Dancing with Change

Change is constant and there is no way to avoid it. Therefore, it is important to have the tools to manage it in order to live a life of harmony. The inability to adapt to changes will result in getting lost in the process and missing out on opportunities.

Change is the act or process of making something different. It is uncomfortable for most people because it requires resilience to adapt to new ways of thinking and doing. The change demands actions, so it is important to take the lead in the change process with confidence. Change will take control of the situation unless it is expected, identified, controlled and mastered. That is, if you don't take control of change, it will take control of you.

Many mums experience a significant amount of

change from the time they become pregnant to the time they decide to return to work.

The degree of change that mums go through differs from mum to mum. However, the significance of this change is universal, as you will remain a mum for the rest of your life.

Now, there are a number of changes that affect mums, most of which begin during the post-birth months. These changes affect body image, relationships, and return-to-work plans.

For example, as we have shared in the previous chapters, return-to-work mums have to learn how to adapt to the working environment, much like a new hire does when joining a new company. The reason for this is that by having a baby, mums have experienced significant changes at home that impact their work lives.

It is expected for return-to-work mums to simply get on with life post-birth without making any noise or disruptions. The changes she has gone through and is going through are rarely discussed in detail because mums are expected to continue with life as if having a baby is easy.

In unmasking the top changes that can occur to mums, we are empowered by the knowledge in preparation for the changes ahead. We are sharing these experiences with you to expose the reality of this transition.

We do this because we don't want mums to fall into the trap of mummy guilt.

By the end of this chapter, you will understand the kind of changes mums go through post-birth and how to manage them for better outcomes.

Baby and Me

As we've shared in previous chapters, there are a lot of mums who suffer in silence once the excitement of pregnancy turns into having to care wholeheartedly for the cute baby in their arms.

Some mums will crave their "old life". That is, the life they had when they were only responsible for themselves and nobody else. Then they will feel mummy guilt for thinking this way because "what kind of mum thinks of a life without her precious baby?"

When mums are thrown into their new lives without much information on what it will feel like to be a new mum, feelings of being out of control and lack of focus can present themselves. In return, they may experience an inability to think positively when they are with their baby. Despite the number of positive supporters (connections) around them, it can be a deeply isolating experience.

There is only one way to manage these feelings and that is to be ready for the change ahead before the change overtakes you.

Understanding these changes and knowing how to manage them is important because it keeps the mum in a positive frame of mind to enjoy her life with her baby. Furthermore, it may also deter future feelings of regret that may surface if mums feel like they were not completely present during this period of time with their baby.

The purpose of understanding the changes ahead is to give control to mums so that they don't have to suffer in silence. When attempting to make sense of their feelings by themselves, they fall into a trap of isolation and loneliness, leading them to think that they are alone in the world and that nobody would understand them.

I will share some of the changes that happen to mums during this time because we want mums to be in control and dance the cha-cha with change.

Changes to Expect

Whether you are currently expecting a baby or already have a baby and are returning to work, it is important to know that you have changed. You need to respect these changes in you because they offer an opportunity to set your goals for the future that you want.

Here are the changes you should expect and some tips to encourage you to be in control of them:

Body Changes

When a mum realises that there is no template for a perfect mum, she is free from self-appointed disappointment.

All bodies are different and a lot of women are proud of their baby-bump. The aim is to continue to love your body after giving birth.

During pregnancy, your body is transformed into a maker, carrier and deliverer of life. During the pregnancy stage, some mums have a beautiful glow on their skin; others may not. This glow is not just about the outward appearance of beauty. It also includes the feeling of confidence that leads one to exude beauty from within.

After giving birth, it is common to have gained weight. Some mums will not fit into their pre-pregnancy clothes, while others will. For those of us who gained weight during pregnancy, we need high motivation levels and commitment if weight loss is to be achieved.

Accept that Your Looks Have Changed

You might experience weight loss, weight gain, sagging body parts, or loss of movement.

The aim is to take control of your body, and if you desire something different, do something to drive the changes that you want to achieve.

Be Objective about What You Want to Achieve
Establish SMARTER goals when trying to achieve any form of physical improvement or body modification.

Be Realistic About What You Are Trying to Achieve
This means that there is no point in setting unrealistic targets because you will ultimately not achieve the desired outcome. It is better to be realistic about setting proper targets for success.

If You Ask for Advice, Be Prepared to Graciously Accept What Is Served
Understand that you can't be sensitive about responses to your questions. For example, if you asked for someone's opinion, you may not like the response, but it's their opinion, and you asked for it.

Do Something that You Enjoy
For example, if you enjoy going for a walk, go out and do it. Keep active as much as possible.

The same applies to any other activity or hobby that makes you feel better.

Don't Try to Fit into the Old Clothes that You No Longer Fit Into
I know it can be frustrating when you try to fit into jeans that are now three sizes smaller than your

current frame. Try motivating yourself into action if you want to fit into those jeans again.

Don't throw out or give away these clothes either – not yet. If you want to, you'll fit into them again.

It is important to realise that you are in complete control of your entire being, all the time.

Sleeping Habits

My physician once told me that lack of sleep can mimic signs of depression. During this time, your attention span will be tested and you will not feel like yourself without adequate sleep.

It is an absolute given that your baby will affect your sleep. If you enjoy sleeping on your own terms and at your own time, be prepared to not have this luxury for a long time.

The reason for sleep disruptions is that babies have their own sleeping needs and unique habits.

Some mums implement structured sleep routines for the baby in the hope that they will have control of their time. While these routines may work for some babies, they do not work for all.

Do not be tempted to believe that all babies will adapt to an established routine or that you will have control over this. It can become a frustrating experience when mums feel like they are failing if the baby does not adhere to a pre-determined sleeping routine.

If, during the first three months of the baby's life, you are able to get four hours of sleep in one stretch, consider yourself lucky, as most mums do not have this luxury.

How to Remain Focused

1. **Accept that you will not sleep soundly for a very long time.**
   When the baby is sleeping, you should also try to rest or sleep. If you can't sleep while the baby is having a nap, simply rest and do as little as possible to reserve your energy for the day and night ahead.

   That being said, some mums profess to having changed their sleeping patterns to align with their baby's needs.

2. **Remind yourself that this stage will pass.**
   One day in the future, you will be able to sleep on your own terms. Your baby will be older and more independent. Once the baby has the ability to walk and talk, they will have a more predictable sleep pattern, which should afford you more sleep time.

3. **Don't believe all the routine books.**
   For me, we established a routine that worked for us.

   While sleep-routine books can provide a good guide for what to expect, don't believe that all babies will follow the same routine.

   Go with your baby's needs because trying to fit a baby into a sleep routine is frustrating. You can avoid all the frustrations and just go with the flow.

   Midwives have told me that if your baby does not nap, it's absolutely okay because the baby will sleep when needed.

4. **Use your connections.**
   It is helpful to use your connections (it could be your SO or another family member) to look after your baby while you have rest.

5. **Rest when you are feeling tired.**
   This is obvious. However, it is common for mothers I have coached to share with me how many accidents they could have avoided if they'd had enough rest. It is understandable that perhaps you don't want to miss out on your baby's activities. However, if you are extremely tired, it is safer to rest; otherwise, accidents might happen.

6. **Don't compare your baby's sleep pattern to anyone else's.**
   There are babies who naturally sleep in a more predictable pattern than others. If you come across a mum whose baby sleeps through the night at six weeks old, it's not a reflection of what you are doing wrong. It's just that babies are different and have different needs.

   We know that your baby will disturb your sleep, and there is simply no way to avoid this. Rest assured that it does get easier to manage, as the baby will eventually establish a more predictable sleep pattern.

Distribution of Duties

It is a fact that all mums change when the baby arrives. In addition to the change in mums, their SOs change, too, during this period.

It is common for new mums to feel that they are responsible for more childcare duties than their SO. Typically, a mum might say that her SO does not have to wake up in the middle of the night to nurse the baby. Or that her SO does not spend as much time with the baby as she does.

In defence of the SO, sometimes there is little he can do when their baby wakes up to nurse on the breast. Similarly, when he goes off to work, it is not to escape baby duties; it is simply the need to go to work and earn money for the family. While we know that the distribution of duties during this phase may be largely unequal, it is possible to implement a fairer system.

For example, on your SO's days off, make it his priority to look after your baby while you busy yourself with other activities. You can do this by focusing on what can be done rather than what is not being done. As an idea, before the baby is born, you could discuss this topic together, and be accountable for the distribution of duties to avoid miscommunication and resentment.

How to Plan for the Baby

1. **Know that the baby will require all of your attention all day, every day.**
   Babies cry, and some do so all the time. A baby's cry is one of the most disturbing sounds to the human ear, and nature intended it to be this way for survival. When a baby is in a crying mood, keep calm and nurse your baby. Trust your instincts. If you think there is something causing the crying, investigate the cause and try to resolve it. Obviously, if there is something serious that is causing the crying, seek medical attention.

   Ensure that your SO knows how to calm and nurse your baby so that this responsibility is not solely yours to manage.

2. **Your SO will have his own style of looking after your baby.**
   Be respectful of your SO's different style. For example, he may have a different manner of holding the bottle to feed your baby. This is okay. Praise your SO for taking care of your baby. If you criticise him for his style of looking after your baby, it may cause unnecessary friction and negatively impact his self-confidence.

3. **Mum first.**
   Accept that your SO may be less involved in caring for the baby than you. Don't resent him for this. You can get him to do more by simply encouraging him to take care of your baby from the very beginning.

   Share the baby chores by delegating activities; for example, bath time could be between your SO and your baby, without you there.

   My physician once told me that it is not only mums who go through post-partum anxiety. Fathers can go through post-partum anxiety, too. Disruptive changes can occur when the baby joins the family. Therefore, it is wise to expect that couples will experience friction as they adapt to their new life with the baby. The goal is to be aware of these disruptive changes so that you can take control of your new lifestyle with confidence. Practise being calm even in stressful situations in order to stay in control of these disruptive situations.

Return-to-Work Changes

A number of mums have difficulty thriving in the corporate world after the baby is born because of the following hurdles:

1. The changes that she has to manage at home.
2. Leading her personal transformation.
3. The stigma attached to return-to-work mums.

One of the most ubiquitous biases is that a mum will be less than capable of delivering results compared to her colleagues without children. It is believed that this disadvantage is brought on by additional responsibilities at home, lack of self-awareness and commitment to work. Of course, we know that this is not always true for everyone.

However, this stigma leads to pressure on return-to-work mums, challenging them to speed up their transformation and demonstrate their capabilities.

We all have a social responsibility to make this stigma redundant by increasing awareness about the challenges of return-to-work mums and then participating in activities that increase the engagement levels, retention rates and opportunities for promotion of return-to-work mums. After all, baby is not a hurdle for performance at work; we need to acknowledge the fact that there are many return-to-work mums who are excellent team players and deliver outstanding business results.

As we know, the increase in the workforce participation rate of return-to-work mums brings increased competition for jobs and more women are now completing higher levels of education and jobs. Therefore, companies that invest in the attraction and retention of return-to-work mums have the distinct advantage of being able to tap into a strong and capable talent base.

Supporting Frameworks

There are a number of change frameworks available online, and most of these include the process to embed change.

Here is a change diagram that I follow to help me to navigate change. I use this to enable me to take the change-leader position by pre-empting and responding to changes, depending on my environment and desires.

This Change Planning Cycle can start at any point. However, for you to lead change, it is advisable to begin with defining the expected changes ahead. This is so you are prepared for what's coming up and can plan accordingly for what resources you may need to drive the change. When you reach the point of action, you will have the tools to live in the change and assess how satisfied you are with what's happening. It is at this point that you can redefine your plans to give you what you want to achieve.

It is important to continuously measure your progress and celebrate your achievements.

Let's Reflect on this Topic
Change is inevitable and its impact on mums is significant.

Being aware of these changes will empower mums to know how to lead change with confidence and avoid mum guilt.

This leads us to our next chapter, which explores dealing with loss and the no-tears approach that helps new mums to overcome loneliness.

Chapter 9

Career Transitions and Life Gems

Mastering Transitions

It is true that job changes can happen at any time, to anyone, including mums on maternity leave.

Whether the job change is due to resignation or employer-led termination, the outcome of this change can be stressful.

Being prepared for career transitions during maternity leave provides a fantastic opportunity for mums to return to the workforce in a different role, to learn new skills to pivot into an entirely different industry, or perhaps to be able to focus on passion projects.

Whatever it is that you decide to do, you are in control. It's your life and your passion.

By the end of this chapter, you will know what to do when your career changes during maternity leave. This knowledge may inspire you to think more broadly about your purpose, what you want to achieve, and how to go about achieving what it is you are passionate about.

The ultimate goal is for you to live your best life. The life that motivates you to work hard and create your desired outcomes.

Unemployment can be devastating for a family. This is because it results in a loss of income. Loss of income can affect the family's financial security – the ability to pay the rent, buy food, afford education and so on.

In addition to the financial impact of unemployment, the emotional toll can be equally devastating. Fear can lead to anger and anger can lead to negative relationships.

It is only through preparation, setting clear goals and planning for the future that we can cushion the effects of career transition during maternity leave.

It is safe to say that nobody's job is secure forever. Therefore, it's best to plan for change rather than to wait for change to happen.

This is the reason preparation is critical for career mums, both before and after having the baby. Planning to have a baby is not always feasible – sometimes it is gifted without planning. However, it is important to always be prepared for your career, finances, and future purpose as soon as you know that your baby is coming.

This level of preparation is critical in ensuring that mums avoid being unprepared in the event of a career transition.

One of the most common topics that mums I coach come to see me about is career transition during maternity leave. This is because they have utilised their time away from work to reflect on their careers and reassess their future.

On the other hand, there are mums who decide not to go back to work in the same company. Sometimes, the employers decide to terminate the employment contract during maternity leave. Let us identify these scenarios in detail.

Resignation

There are a number of mums who decide to not return to work after maternity leave. These mums inform their bosses that they can no longer return to work for a variety of reasons.

These reasons may include:
- The mum prefers to stay at home to look after the baby.

- Childcare costs exceed the income the mum would earn.
- The family decides that the mum does not need to work anymore.
- The mum was not engaged at work before having the baby.
- The mum cannot achieve the expectations of the job.
- The mum wants to focus on a new career path.
- The mum wants to focus on other creative avenues.

Employer-led Termination

As an employee, it is up to us to ensure that our skills and knowledge are relevant and valued in the workplace, so we can be as secure as possible in our role.

Although many workplaces offer paid and unpaid maternity-leave provisions, by and large, the provisions range from a few weeks to less than twelve months.

Some of the reasons for employer-led terminations during maternity leave are:
- Company restructuring.
- Business closing down.

At any point in time, mums can decide not to return to work after maternity leave, and no employee is immune to changes in the business landscape. Therefore, it is important to have career goals established either before maternity leave or during it, so that you are prepared for any career changes that may happen in the future.

I will now discuss a few scenarios and explore the steps in each of them to prepare you for your career and life plan either before or after the baby. The important points to remember are the need to create your goals and then undertake actionable steps to activate them.

Returning to Work?

A lot of women I have coached did not return to the exact same job they had before their baby was born. This is because they realised that the baby had provided them with the opportunity to do something they really love, rather than work just to earn money. Or that their skills are required in another role within the business.

Some of these women even started their own businesses and worked odd hours to align with the baby's routine. Their feedback about this transition was that while the financial returns were not as high as those they received in their corporate job, the job satisfaction was far greater. Plus, they got to save some money on childcare fees, so their household expenses decreased.

On the other hand, there are women who returned to

a different job because they were given the opportunity to do so and they seized these opportunities.

However, there are some mums who feel that they have no choice but to return to the same job because of financial responsibilities. It could be because they are the primary "breadwinner". Therefore, these mums need to continue to work to financially support their families. Sometimes, these mums resent having to return to work, but when they accept their responsibility, they are able to persevere and continue to do what they have to do.

Whatever you decide to do is completely up to you and your circumstances.

What to do in times of career change?
When you realise that you've reached a fork in your career, these are the steps to follow to ensure that you remain confident and focused on the future:

1. **Take care of yourself.**
   It is easy to let the stress of career transitions impact your self-esteem. Don't let it. Get off the couch, have a shower, brush your hair. Try not to focus on the reasons for the change; it is irrelevant now. Do focus on what you want to do. Do you want to work again? Do you want to pursue further education? Where would you like to work? What type of work would you like to do?

By taking care of yourself, you regain your confidence and increase your ability to focus on and plan for your future.

2. **Create goals.**
   Define what you want to do using SMARTER goals. Share your goals with your connections, and perhaps they can give you other opportunities that align with your goals.

   In my experience, connections enjoy supporting you because people want to be aligned to motivated people. Therefore, if your connections trust in you and your abilities, they will support you, and your goals.

3. **Enjoy yourself.**
   Whether it's taking your baby for a walk out in the fresh air or writing in your journal, do the things that you enjoy doing. The more enjoyment you get out of your day, the more positive your outlook will be. A positive outlook is important because your connections will most likely want to support people who are confident and focused rather than those who lack energy.

4. **Your new job is finding your purpose.**
   Whether you are looking to get back into the workforce or carving a new path, finding your

purpose begins by understanding what your purpose is. There is no right or wrong answer. You just need to make an agreement within yourself, for yourself.

If your purpose is to be employed, then work on your CV, connect with your connections and define your value proposition for your future employer.

In my experience, a lot of jobs are secured through connections, so it's important to stay connected with your connections.

If you are branching out into something new, make it worthwhile by understanding why you want to do this and how aligned it is to your purpose.

For example, if you choose to learn how to speak a new language, well done. But you need to truly understand what the purpose of this is and how it can benefit you in your future role.

5. **Be good and ignore toxics.**
   Surround yourself with good people. You may want to use this time to appreciate yourself for everything that you have accomplished.

   Be aware that there are people you know who will not celebrate your success. They won't even be interested in what you are passionate about. There is no point in trying to impress these people, as they can detract from your goals.

As I have detailed in earlier chapters, it is important to distance yourself from toxic people during this time. And it's equally important to not be toxic to others.

Present a positive outlook despite your challenges; be polite to others despite your frustrations; be calm despite your insecurity. People will remember your strength of character, and this will provide a springboard for your future success.

Career plans and life goals require your time, effort, energy and commitment in order to bring them to life. It may be challenging at first to access your inner thoughts. You can start by practising meditation on a regular basis to reach deeper levels of self-awareness and allowing yourself to be guided by your thoughts and visions for your future.

Once you have defined your goals and planned them accordingly, maternity leave will be an amazing opportunity to direct your life towards the path that you have created.

Bea's Story

There are times in life when, despite all of our planning and goal setting, the unexpected happens. Therefore, it is important to be ready for the unexpected.

Thirty-eight-year-old Bea was a psychologist at a local primary public school. The school was in the rougher side of town, where unemployment was high and single-parent families were the norm.

Bea had been working at this school for four years. She had been bored with her job for the past two years, but having two children at home and a husband who worked on a temporary basis in the IT industry did not provide their family the financial security that Bea wanted.

Bea comes from an upper middle-class family, and both her mother and father worked in the healthcare industry. Bea grew up without knowing about financial difficulties and job insecurity.

Bea's husband, Will, had lost his job the previous year when his company relocated their entire operations overseas. A number of companies relocated overseas during this time to decrease the cost of business.

Bea and Will did not expect that Will would struggle to secure a job, as he was a very capable expert in his domain. However, Will's options in securing another role were limited due to the seniority of his previous role and a limited number of suitable vacancies in the market.

Will decided to continue to work in consulting roles, mainly sourced and secured through his connections.

When Bea came to see me, she said that she was twelve weeks pregnant. She was emotional and contemplated having an abortion because she and Will could not afford to have another baby.

Bea said that she felt like a failure and she was so tired of just trying to make ends meet. She said that she and Will hardly spoke to each other anymore because their focus over the past three years had been on looking after the two kids.

Quietly, Bea also wanted to find another job, but her plans had to be put on hold because she knew that her job was the only financial security that the family had. The feeling of being the breadwinner made her feel nervous and distracted her from planning for the future.

Bea was my client for three months and during this time she was able to:

1. **Focus on her needs and develop her career transition plan.**
   Eventually, Bea accepted a job with a private clinic, which came along with a 20% salary increase. Her new job not only provided a higher income but also higher levels of job satisfaction as she enjoyed working with a greater variety of clients.

2. **Organise her finances to provide her with the security that she needed.**
   Bea and Will partnered with an accountant who helped them to better understand their financial situation, which was not as desperate as Bea had initially thought. This provided a sense of relief and comfort. They both worked on developing a reasonable budget, and with Bea's increased income, they were able to save some money for the new addition to their family.

3. **Reposition her self-image.**
   Bea stopped calling herself a loser and focused on her winning qualities, which were being a great mum, a supportive wife, a good friend, and a capable psychologist.

What you need to keep in mind is that transitions cause chaos. It is difficult to focus on goals in an environment where chaos dominates. So, develop your transition plans and use your time to continue to be the you that you want to be.

Believe that you can and you will.

In Summary

Career transitions can happen to anyone and being on maternity leave is a great time to take the lead in driving career transitions and discover your life's purpose in order to live the life of your dreams.

Don't let transitions drive your actions. Act first by planning and by setting your life goals.

Determine your purpose. Define what you want to achieve and how. Use the SMARTER goal framework for your ideas and activation plans.

This is the best way to take control of your world and create the life that you want.

This leads us to the next chapter, where we will talk about the future woman. This woman is the expert of herself. She is not afraid to fall down while chasing after her dreams because she gets right back up again and runs after them with unwavering determination. She stares at her challenges and studies them so that she knows how to overpower them. She is a winner. She is boss mum.

Chapter 10

Boss Mum

I'm so proud of her

The boss mum is the boss of her life. She is confident in her purpose and makes her decisions accordingly. She does not allow mum guilt to paralyse her ambitions or stifle her progress. She is authentic, kind, generous with her time and takes the lead in dancing the cha-cha with changes.

This mum doesn't play by the rules that others have set for her life because she knows that sometimes, these rules are not applicable to her and do not suit her purpose. Therefore, she creates her own rules, which are aligned to her purpose, and by doing so, she lives the life of her dreams, not a life that she just puts up with when she wakes from her slumber.

Everyone has the power to be anyone they want to

be. I will show you how easy it is to live the life that you want, despite all the obstacles.

The ability to live the life that you love is yours when you allow yourself to destroy the mental blocks that stop you from believing it is possible. The mental blocks are called limiting beliefs.

Limiting beliefs are based on thoughts that you create in your mind; they tell you that you can't achieve what you want to because you are either too old, or you don't have enough experience, or you don't have enough time, et cetera. You have the power to overcome these limiting beliefs simply by recognising that they exist and that they can't exist without you.

In this chapter, I will demonstrate ways to overcome your limiting beliefs. I will show you how you can live the life that you love because you deserve it. There's no reason you should stop yourself from moving forward to achieve your goals.

Have you ever stopped yourself from applying for a promotion because you didn't think you had enough experience? Or, worse still, because the job advertisement listed ten desired skills and you thought you only had some of them to offer? And, later on, you discovered that someone with less experience got the job?

Ultimately, the person who applies for the job has a significant advantage over the person who did not apply. As the saying goes, "You have to be in it to win it."

The limiting belief that prevented you from submitting your CV is the same limiting belief that prevents you from starting your own business or writing your book. Overcoming limiting beliefs is important to living the life that you love because it is only with courage and through action that your goals can be realised.

Everybody has complete control over the quality of the life that they live. If you disagree with this statement, please consider what limiting beliefs you have that prevent you from believing this and then reflect on why these limiting beliefs exist and how you can overcome them to create a path towards your desired life.

In order to live the life that you love, you need courage because you will make mistakes in the journey and these mistakes should not stop you from moving forward. For example, you may have incorrectly assessed a particular situation, the outcome of which was not desired. These are all improvement opportunities. They lead to increased self-awareness, which, in turn, leads to knowing the impact that you have on others.

Here are some steps you need to practise to live the life that you love.

1. **Become aware.**
   Love the person you are and visualise the person that you want to be. Exude positive energy, and be poised at all times. Be kind to yourself and generous with your time when it comes to your connections.

   You need to know who you are. Be clear about who you are, who you want to be and what you are doing for yourself to be the person that you aspire to be.

   Be realistic about your goals so that you remain authentic to yourself. If you try to be someone you are not, it will not be a sustainable, positive change.

   The only way that you can transform yourself into the person that you want to be is through action. This means that you need to work towards mastering transitions while continually measuring your progress.

2. **Motivate yourself to set and achieve your goals.**
   The word motivation is derived from the word motive, which refers to your needs and desires. Motivation is the process of stimulation of action to accomplish needs and desires. Motivation requires effort and energy, particularly when positioned towards a goal.

Most goals have innate challenges. It is important to remain focused on the end-goal so as not to lose traction as you move towards achievement.

Your goals are created by you and for you. Therefore, do not lose motivation when you are on the journey towards achieving them. Achieving your goals can be incredibly fulfilling and addictive. You will most likely set additional goals for yourself once you have achieved one set of goals. This level of continuous self-improvement is what makes boss mums love their lives.

3. **Be accountable.**
Accountability means being responsible. You are the sole architect and owner of your goals. Therefore, you are completely responsible for achieving them.

There will be times when you feel that your goals are not achievable because of a particular situation or person. Acknowledge the possibility that these thoughts might be limiting beliefs that you have created for yourself.

Take responsibility for challenging these limiting beliefs. It is only when you have a clear understanding of these thoughts that you can continue to progress towards achieving your goals.

On the journey to being boss mum, you are the

only authority. Own your goals and motivate yourself to overcome the challenges you will encounter along the way.

The outcome of your perseverance will be the knowledge that you have accomplished your goals and strengthened your commitment to your future goals.

4. **Be a great connection.**
People want to be connected with like-minded people. When you are energised to action, you are motivated and confident and you will most likely attract the same type of people.

Leverage the skills and capabilities of the people in your network who have a positive influence on you. Open yourself up to the opportunities to learn from others and support others when appropriate. For example, I know of a number of boss mums who mentor and coach people. Through coaching others, they also increase their professional profile and good reputation.

5. **Happiness isn't all about the money.**
If your life of passion is not about earning money, that's okay. Plenty of happy people are not motivated by financial returns. For them, they derive satisfaction through owning their time, not having to stress about pleasing others, being able to cry

when they want to and swear from time to time without the risk of offending anyone.

The Traits of a Boss Mum

The boss mum does not let mum guilt overpower her because she is confident that she gives her best all the time.

The boss mum is in control of her life, and she is on a journey of continuous self-improvement. She is aware of herself and her environment. She is focused on her goals and motivated by bringing her visions to life. She knows that she alone has the power to transform her life. She celebrates her successes and uses her failures as a footstool towards better opportunities.

Being the boss mum begins with living the life you love and loving the person that you are. Be confident that your ideas and decisions are perfect, and when they are not, it's okay, because you have the power to change the direction of your path anytime.

We are all boss mums, and when we decide to throw away the heavy, useless baggage that we all once carried, life feels great.

One of my most memorable clients is Julie.

Julie was older than me and had more life experience than I had but these differences did not have an impact on our Coach and Client relationship.

Julie was a school teacher who had devoted her entire working life to teaching primary school children.

Last year, Julie's husband, Bob, passed away unexpectedly in a horrific road accident, in which Bob became a casualty as he was standing on the curb, waiting to cross the road. A truck collided with a car and the car was flung onto the curb where Bob was standing.

Julie and Bob were married for over forty years, and when Bob passed away, Julie felt alone and reflected on her relationship with their only daughter, Mary. Mary had been estranged from her and Bob for many years.

Julie shared with me that even when Mary was a baby, she struggled to have a maternal connection with her only child. Back then, she did not have anyone to speak to about her feelings of emotional disconnection from her child. Julie said that she was an emotionally distant mother and Mary spent more quality time with Bob's mother (Mary's grandmother) than she did with her.

Therefore, it was not surprising that once Mary was old enough to leave the home, she did so without much fuss, and ultimately, as years went by, the connection between mother and daughter became more estranged.

Julie said that it was only in Bob's passing that she felt the strong urge to reconnect with Mary. Unfortunately, she did not have any means to reach out to her. It was by chance that one of her friends from church was able to find Mary online, where she informed Mary about her father's passing.

When Julie came to see me, it had been over a week since Bob was laid to rest. Julie said that she was optimistic about the future of the relationship between her and Mary as they continued to be in contact and support each other through their grieving process.

I asked her what had led to the distance between her and her only child and Julie said that in the past, she didn't know how to be a mother.

What Julie wanted now, more than ever, was to grieve for Bob, overcome the regret she felt for the type of mother she was, strengthen her relationship with her daughter and be a loving grandmother to her two grandchildren (Mary's kids).

These significant changes in Julie's life required action.

Julie started by clarifying her purpose. She felt relieved once she defined this because she regained control over her future. Then she defined her goals.

She realised that for so long, her goals had been connected to Bob's goals, so it was a new experience for her to have to set goals for herself and to be completely accountable for them.

Julie and I had eight sessions and then she told me that she was planning to relocate to live closer to Mary.

Julie's passion to live a life that she loves was stronger than the obstacles and challenges life had put ahead of her.

Julie's story proves that if you are determined to live the life that you love, there is nothing in the world that can get in the way of achieving your goals, not even your past.

Start living the life that you love by practising and applying the steps in this book. The only thing you will regret is not activating your life soon enough.

Boss mums are on the rise, and together, we will achieve our goals.

To this End
Your life is yours; therefore, you alone have the power to make it the life that you love. Limiting beliefs are beliefs that prevent you from living on your own terms. Challenge these limiting beliefs and live the life that you love.

Everyone has some challenges in life. The difference in our challenges is how we interpret them and what actions we take to overcome them. All challenges are designed to be overpowered.

I am happy that you have almost made it to the end of the book. I now welcome you to read the final chapter. This chapter is a summary of everything in this book and you can use it to springboard your life into the life that you love.

So, relax, take a deep breath, and turn to the next page.

Chapter 11

Conclusion

You, yourself, as much as anybody in the entire universe, deserve your love and affection.
—**Buddha**

Everything begins with self-love. Knowing what this means and how to use it in daily life is the key to successful living. It is neither selfish nor unexpected to love yourself first before you can focus on loving others, baby included.

The career woman works hard and invests in her career. When a working woman has a baby, it does not mean that her career has come to an end. In some ways, this experience can enhance her entire career experience, thus leading to a more fulfilled life.

Remember, being a mother is a significant role. It is a lifelong commitment to giving yourself wholeheartedly to another human, which makes motherhood the best gift that anyone can be blessed with.

There are many challenges that life brings us and when we are presented with these challenges, we have choices to make: to either transform, be static or ignore the situation. We might even unwittingly ignore the opportunities.

The career mum can balance motherhood and career with confidence and determination. She knows how to overcome challenges and seize opportunities.

To have it all means different things to different people. The outcome relies on the perspective that you have.

Ultimately, what we can all agree on is that women can successfully manage both motherhood and career at the same time. We know that challenges are a constant and that our ability to respond to these challenges is the differentiator between those who succeed in living life as they desire and those who do not.

I hope that you are inspired by the stories that you have read in this book, and most importantly, love yourself and live your life on your terms.

Finally, now that you have all the tools for success, use them. Practise on yourself and on other mums

Conclusion

who may call on you for support. Trust yourself and conquer your world – one baby step at a time.

If you would like to connect with me, please visit me at www.alexisdunstan.com.

END

Acknowledgements

This book was brought to life with the encouragement and love of my husband and sons, who believe in the importance of my message to all working mothers.

I would like to thank both Dr Haris Syed, founder of Coach Transformation Academy, for guiding me to be a successful Coach and Moustafa Hamwi, founder of Passionpreneur Publishing for his support throughout my Author's journey.

Finally, to all the working mothers who devote their lives towards strengthening their families and careers – may we continue to deliver a positive impact at home and in the workplace today and into the future.

Alexis Dunstan is an Australian Professional Certified Coach (International Coach Federation), a wife, and a mum of two sons. Her expertise is in coaching mothers in business.

Alexis began her coaching career in Dubai, United Arab Emirates, where she lived and worked for a number of years as a Coach and Human Resources Leader.

Alexis is passionate about partnering with working mothers to identify and overcome the hurdles that are placed in the path of all working mothers.

Alexis has earned a double Master's degree in Business Administration and Human Resources Management and is a certified Neuro-linguistic Program Coach and Trainer.

www.ingramcontent.com/pod-product-compliance
Lightning Source LLC
Chambersburg PA
CBHW071619080526
44588CB00010B/1194